Edited by Naomi Starkey May–August 2015

New Daylight © BRF 2015

The Bible Reading Fellowship
15 The Chambers, Vineyard, Abingdon OX14 3FE
Tel: 01865 319700; Fax: 01865 319701
E-mail: enquiries@brf.org.uk; Website: www.brf.org.uk

ISBN 978 0 85746 127 8

Distributed in Australia by Mediacom Education Inc., PO Box 610, Unley, SA 5061.
Tel: 1800 811 311; Fax: 08 8297 8719;
E-mail: admin@mediacom.org.au
Available also from all good Christian bookshops in Australia.
For individual and group subscriptions in Australia:
Mrs Rosemary Morrall, PO Box W35, Wanniassa, ACT 2903.

Distributed in New Zealand by Scripture Union Wholesale, PO Box 760, Wellington
Tel: 04 385 0421; Fax: 04 384 3990; E-mail: suwholesale@clear.net.nz

Publications distributed to more than 60 countries

Acknowledgments
The New Revised Standard Version of the Bible, Anglicised Edition, copyright © 1989, 1995 by the
Division of Christian Education of the National Council of the Churches of Christ in the USA.
Used by permission. All rights reserved.

The Holy Bible, New International Version, Anglicised edition, copyright © 1979, 1984, 2011 by
Biblica. Used by permission of Hodder & Stoughton Publishers, an Hachette UK company. All
rights reserved. 'NIV' is a registered trademark of Biblica. UK trademark number 1448790.

Extracts from the Authorised Version of the Bible (The King James Bible), the rights in which
are vested in the Crown, are reproduced by permission of the Crown's Patentee, Cambridge
University Press.

The Revised Common Lectionary is copyright © The Consultation on Common Texts, 1992 and is
reproduced with permission. *The Christian Year: Calendar, Lectionary and Collects*, which includes
the *Common Worship* lectionary (the Church of England's adaptations of the *Revised Common
Lectionary*, published as the Principal Service lectionary) is copyright © The Central Board of
Finance of the Church of England, 1995, 1997, and material from it is reproduced with
permission.

Printed by Gutenberg Press, Tarxien, Malta.

Suggestions for using *New Daylight*

Find a regular time and place, if possible, where you can read and pray undisturbed. Before you begin, take time to be still and perhaps use the BRF prayer. Then read the Bible passage slowly (try reading it aloud if you find it over-familiar), followed by the comment. You can also use *New Daylight* for group study and discussion, if you prefer.

The prayer or point for reflection can be a starting point for your own meditation and prayer. Many people like to keep a journal to record their thoughts about a Bible passage and items for prayer. In *New Daylight* we also note the Sundays and some special festivals from the Church calendar, to keep in step with the Christian year.

New Daylight and the Bible

New Daylight contributors use a range of Bible versions, and you will find a list of the versions used opposite, on page 2. You are welcome to use your own preferred version alongside the passage printed in the notes. This can be particularly helpful if the Bible text has been abridged.

New Daylight affirms that the whole of the Bible is God's revelation to us, and we should read, reflect on and learn from every part of both Old and New Testaments. Usually the printed comment presents a straight-forward 'thought for the day', but sometimes it may also raise questions rather than simply providing answers, as we wrestle with some of the more difficult passages of Scripture.

New Daylight *is also available in a deluxe edition (larger format). Visit your local Christian bookshop or contact the BRF office, who can also give details about a cassette version for the visually impaired. For a Braille edition, contact St John's Guild, Sovereign House, 12–14 Warwick Street, Coventry CV5 6ET.*

Comment on *New Daylight*

To send feedback, you may email or write to BRF at the addresses shown opposite. If you would like your comment to be included on our website, please email connect@brf.org.uk. You can also Tweet to @brfonline, using the hashtag #brfconnect.

Writers in this issue

Margaret Silf is an ecumenical Christian, committed to working across and beyond the denominational divides. She devotes herself to writing and accompanying others on their spiritual journey.

Barbara Mosse is a retired Anglican priest with experience in various chaplaincies. A freelance lecturer and retreat giver, she is the author of *The Treasures of Darkness* (Canterbury Press, 2003), *Encircling the Christian Year* (BRF, 2012) and *Welcoming the Way of the Cross* (BRF, 2013).

Tony Horsfall is a freelance trainer and retreat leader based in Yorkshire, with his own ministry, Charis Training. He is an elder of Ackworth Community Church and has written several books for BRF, his latest being *Deep Calls to Deep*.

Rosemary Lain-Priestley has been a priest in the Church of England for 18 years. She is an advocate for the ministries and flourishing of female clergy. She is also the author of three books and the mother of three children.

Ian Adams is a poet, writer, photographer and priest working with themes of spirituality, culture and community. He is the creator of Morning Bell (Twitter @pacebene), and author of *Running Over Rocks* (Canterbury Press, 2013). He is an Associate Missioner with Fresh Expressions and leads the Missional Communities, Orders and Projects hub at CMS.

Veronica Zundel is an Oxford graduate, writer and journalist. She lives with her husband and son in North London, where they belong to the Mennonite Church.

David Winter is retired from parish ministry. An honorary Canon of Christ Church, Oxford, he is well known as a writer and broadcaster. His most recent book for BRF is *At the End of the Day*.

Fiona Stratta is a qualified speech and language therapist and speech and drama teacher, working with adults and children. She is the author of *Walking with Old Testament Women* (BRF, 2015).

Andrew Jones is Archdeacon of Meirionnydd in the Diocese of Bangor. He has written *Pilgrimage: the journey to remembering our story* (BRF, 2011 and *Mary: a Gospel witness to transfiguration and liberation* (BRF, 2014).

Naomi Starkey writes...

Have you been Skyped? Thanks to the internet and Skype software, it is now possible not only to speak (for free) to somebody on the far side of the world but to see their face too. The media revolution of the past couple of decades has transformed communication in many ways but, at the same time, has opened up new pitfalls—as many learn to their cost! A late night email, hastily written and sent, can sound much more harsh, flippant or plain rude than intended, when it is re-read the following morning.

Misunderstanding is more of a risk when we can't detect the 'tone of voice' of the writer, and it can be even more of a challenge when we are reading things written in a very different place and time. In this issue of *New Daylight*, we have a fascinating set of readings from David Winter, exploring how we can misunderstand the Bible. Including some very popular and much-loved passages, he reflects on how we can fail to get to the deeper meaning of familiar words—or misread them altogether.

It goes without saying that the task of discerning the deeper (and correct) meaning of what we read in the Bible is a vital one, although it may take more than a bit of work and may, even then, not be something we can establish beyond question. That is why we will never come to the end of what we can learn from the Bible, even from parts that we think we know very well, providing we come each time with hearts open and alert to the inspiration of God's Spirit.

Over the next four months we continue with our exploration of John's Gospel, with contributions from Margaret Silf, Tony Horsfall and Veronica Zundel covering two chapters apiece, while Ian Adams takes a similarly in-depth approach to the Servant Songs in the book of Isaiah. I am pleased to introduce a new contributor in this issue: Rosemary Lain-Priestley, a London-based priest, writer and broadcaster. Her readings on 'Significant women of the scriptures' range from Eve to some of the women prominent in the early church and show how much their lives, even if briefly recorded, can teach us. It is also good to welcome Fiona Stratta to *New Daylight*. Fiona has written two books of imaginative studies for Bible meditation, published by BRF: *Walking with Gospel Women* and *Walking with Old Testament Women*.

The BRF Prayer

Almighty God,
you have taught us that your word is a lamp for our feet
and a light for our path. Help us, and all who prayerfully
read your word, to deepen our fellowship with you
and with each other through your love.
And in so doing may we come to know you more fully,
love you more truly, and follow more faithfully
in the steps of your son Jesus Christ, who lives and reigns
with you and the Holy Spirit, one God for evermore.
Amen

Water of life: John 3—4

My daughter and son-in-law were married in a little chapel in the mountains. A relative, a professional church organist and composer, was attending the wedding and they asked him to play the organ for them. He gladly agreed, but, when he was shown the organ, he found that it was in very bad shape, had not been played for years and was unlikely to produce a single note in tune. Of course, he could not let them down at the last minute, however much the dilapidated old organ offended his professional sensibility.

So, the ceremony began and he did his very best to get a recognisable melody out of the instrument. Indeed, it was an unforgettable wedding and we all appreciated the music. When it was over, the minister who had officiated offered his words of congratulation and encouragement to the happy couple, then added a special word of thanks to the organist. 'That old instrument is so battered,' he said, 'but today, sir, you made it sing!'

I could not help remembering this incident as I reflected on the theme of our scriptural journey through the next two weeks. Our relative transformed a battered old organ into music that could sing out and thrill the hearts of all who heard it. Jesus does the same thing on a much grander scale. He too takes us as we are, battered and out of tune, and transforms us. He takes water from the well and directs our attention to another kind of water—the water of life. He takes the complications of a troubled woman's life and transforms them into a power and energy that carries her whole community to a new understanding of who Jesus is. He goes on to show his disciples that the bread they think he must surely need at this noontide hour is, in fact, the bread of life he already possesses in abundance and asks us only to help with the harvest. Finally, he calls forth life from the jaws of death, transforming a father's faith into new life for his son.

All this is offered to us. We are a bit like that tuneless old organ. At Jesus' touch, we too shall sing.

Margaret Silf

The water of rebirth

Now there was a Pharisee named Nicodemus, a leader of the Jews. He came to Jesus by night and said to him, 'Rabbi, we know that you are a teacher who has come from God; for no one can do these signs that you do apart from the presence of God.' Jesus answered him, 'Very truly, I tell you, no one can see the kingdom of God without being born from above.' Nicodemus said to him, 'How can anyone be born after having grown old? Can one enter a second time into the mother's womb and be born?' Jesus answered, 'Very truly, I tell you, no one can enter the kingdom of God without being born of water and Spirit. What is born of the flesh is flesh, and what is born of the Spirit is spirit. Do not be astonished that I said to you, "You must be born from above."'

I love the story of this man Nicodemus who seeks out Jesus by night. He is in a position of authority. It really would not do for him to be seen talking with this radical young teacher who might well prove to be a threat to the status quo. So he goes after dark, quietly and unobserved, in search of the conversation he needs to have.

The conversation takes an unexpected turn, however. Jesus tells him no one can enter the Kingdom without a second birthing experience. Now the literal-minded Nicodemus is out of his depth. What can Jesus mean?

It might help to remind ourselves that every human birth begins with the breaking of the waters—the sudden flood as the amniotic fluid is released. Similarly, each stage of our spiritual journey begins with an outpouring of divine grace. We cannot control it. It may suddenly over-whelm us or gently surprise us, but it initiates a *spiritual* birth, that will bringing that which is of God within us to visible and active life in the world around us. The Holy Spirit is the living water from which our lives in God come forth.

Reflection

May the author of life break the living waters that enfold our embryonic souls and bring to birth in us the fullness of all that we can be.

MARGARET SILF

The water flows where it will

[Jesus said] 'The wind blows where it chooses, and you hear the sound of it, but you do not know where it comes from or where it goes. So it is with everyone who is born of the Spirit.' Nicodemus said to him, 'How can these things be?' Jesus answered him, 'Are you a teacher of Israel, and yet you do not understand these things? Very truly, I tell you, we speak of what we know and testify to what we have seen; yet you do not receive our testimony. If I have told you about earthly things and you do not believe, how can you believe if I tell you about heavenly things?'

Once the waters have broken, the physical process of birth is under way and nothing is going to stop it. Anyone who has given birth knows that, from that moment, the process is not something you can control or micromanage. The baby will arrive in its own time and, when it arrives, you will hold in your arms a new person with a life of his or her own—yours to nourish and sustain, guide and love, but not to control or own.

What applies to physical birth is also true for spiritual rebirth, Jesus tells Nicodemus. Once the Spirit is flowing freely through our lives, the results are not ours to control, although we can see the effects.

My daughter is an obstetrician. She has studied the science of birth extensively; she is also the mother of two little girls. She understands the difference between having the expertise and actually living the experience. To become a parent is to move from theory into mystery. Perhaps this reflects what Jesus is trying to convey to Nicodemus. Even if we knew all there is to know about physical life and how to manage it, we would not even begin to understand the sacred mystery of our souls' rebirth. The living water of the Spirit flows on its own course, with scant regard for our human maps.

Reflection

May we be free of all desire to grasp the living water in our hands, content to let it flow on its own life-giving way through our hearts.

MARGARET SILF

JOHN 3:22–27 (NRSV)

The water that purifies

After this Jesus and his disciples went into the Judean country-side, and he spent some time there with them and baptised. John also was baptising at Aenon near Salim because water was abundant there; and people kept coming and were being baptised—John, of course, had not yet been thrown into prison. Now a discussion about purification arose between John's disciples and a Jew. They came to John and said to him, 'Rabbi, the one who was with you across the Jordan, to whom you testified, here he is baptising, and all are going to him.' John answered, 'No one can receive anything except what has been given from heaven.'

Today we encounter a different kind of living water—the water of baptism. Baptism reflects our need to be reborn into a different dimension of existence. Symbolically we descend into the primeval waters of pre-birth and emerge newborn to begin our conscious journey with God.

Water, however, is not just a symbol of rebirth but also a means of purification. It holds and nurtures us in the womb until we are ready to be born. It cleanses us after we have been born. As soon as a new baby arrives, it is washed, then placed in its mother's arms. Our celebration of baptism captures this process in terms of our spiritual birth. We are symbolically cleansed in its waters, to be held eternally in God's loving arms.

In today's passage we find two baptisers—Jesus and John. Where two people are doing the same thing, there is the potential for dispute. We see what happens when we take our focus away from the real experience of God's cleansing power and concentrate too much on the procedural details. A discussion arises about the nature of purification and whether Jesus is usurping John's authority.

John settles the issue definitively: authority comes from the author of our being, who is God. The living water that cleanses and purifies us comes from God alone. John is merely an instrument through which that grace can flow.

Reflection

As we seek in our own lives to be conduits of God's grace, may we never forget the source from which it flows or seek to claim it as our own.

MARGARET SILF

Rest beside the water

Now when Jesus learned that the Pharisees had heard, 'Jesus is making and baptising more disciples than John'—although it was not Jesus himself but his disciples who baptised—he left Judea and started back to Galilee. But he had to go through Samaria. So he came to a Samaritan city called Sychar, near the plot of ground that Jacob had given to his son Joseph. Jacob's well was there, and Jesus, tired out by his journey, was sitting by the well. It was about noon.

The well is a long-standing and powerful symbol of the source of life. I live near the Peak District in northern England, where many villages maintain the tradition of well-dressing, which involves constructing a tableau, usually representing a Biblical story, using natural materials such as moss, ferns and flower petals. These tableaux, erected beside the village well, were historically constructed in thanksgiving that the village had been spared the ravages of the plague.

In today's passage, Jesus comes upon an ancient well known as Jacob's well, in the hostile territory of Samaria. The age and history of this well grounds the story deep in the story of the people. Jesus himself seeks refreshment from this source, but the living water he will reveal is a gift from God, flowing down through the ages. Jesus rests by the well in his weariness, knowing that what is really needed is living water, which will overflow in a grace that will quench our thirst eternally.

We need this living water, for we are weary, thirsty and seeking respite from the midday sun on our inner journey. Yet, all too often, we are in denial about our needs. We convince ourselves that we can keep going. We take on too many tasks and exhaust ourselves, not stopping to rest our bodies and souls. One of the great gifts of today's scripture for me is the realisation that Jesus also got tired and needed to rest. Tomorrow we will see how much more this well provides for the one who can honestly acknowledge his or her deepest needs.

Reflection

Jesus sits beside Jacob's well to rest. Can we accept his invitation to sit and rest beside him?

MARGARET SILF

11

A challenging conversation

A Samaritan woman came to draw water and Jesus said to her, 'Give me a drink.' (His disciples had gone to the city to buy food.) The Samaritan woman said to him, 'How is it that you, a Jew, ask a drink of me, a woman of Samaria?' (Jews do not share things in common with Samaritans.) Jesus answered her, 'If you knew the gift of God, and who it is that is saying to you, "Give me a drink", you would have asked him, and he would have given you living water.'

In Jesus' time, every village would have had a functional well and it would have been central to the life of the people. It would have been the place to which the women especially would have gravitated each day to draw water for the needs of their families. So, it is no surprise that Jesus stops to rest beside a well. What is surprising is that this well is in hostile territory. Jesus and his friends are passing through Samaria. This is a Samaritan well. To stop here was to make a statement. We shall see, as the story progresses, just how strong that statement was and what the consequences were. What is perhaps even more surprising is that, here at this well, in a staggering display of political incorrectness, Jesus engages in conversation with a woman.

The woman herself can readily see the irony in this situation. Here is a Jew sitting talking with her, a Samaritan, and even asking her for a drink. It would not have been acceptable for a Jew and a Samaritan to share the same cup, let alone cross the gender barrier, but this is no normal situation. Jesus knows who he is talking with and what she really needs. He also knows what will satisfy that deep need, if only she can acknowledge it, first to herself and then to God. He knows that while he is asking her for a drink, she is the one who is dying of a thirst deeper than any ordinary water can assuage.

Reflection

Can you imagine yourself sitting beside Jesus at the well and him asking you, 'What do you really need, in the deepest part of your being?' How might you respond?

MARGARET SILF

At the well without a bucket

> The woman said to him, 'Sir, you have no bucket, and the well is deep. Where do you get that living water? Are you greater than our ancestor Jacob, who gave us the well, and with his sons and his flocks drank from it?' Jesus said to her, 'Everyone who drinks of this water will be thirsty again, but those who drink of the water that I will give them will never be thirsty. The water that I will give will become in them a spring of water gushing up to eternal life.' The woman said to him, 'Sir, give me this water, so that I may never be thirsty or have to keep coming here to draw water.'

I once attended a parish celebration, for which the parishioners had provided a fine feast. In the middle of the table stood a very attractive-looking bowl of rice salad. We all enjoyed the meal, but then, when most of the food was gone, I noticed to my surprise that the bowl of salad had remained untouched. My heart went out to whoever had made it. Why had no one taken any? The answer was not hard to find. There was no spoon. Much as we might have longed to enjoy it, there was no way of accessing it.

The woman at the well poses the same problem to Jesus. He has offered her a drink, but he has no bucket! Actually, of course, it is she— and we—who have the problem, not Jesus. We, too, are thirsty for something we cannot even name, but we have no way of accessing it, even if we do discover it. We have no bucket.

Jesus' response is profoundly simple, yet earth-shatteringly radical. He does not need a bucket, because he is the 'bucket'. He is the one who can open up in us this profound source of life that will satisfy and fulfil our deepest longings. History, however ancient and revered, as in the story of Jacob, cannot achieve this. Nor can dreams of an imagined future. The living water springs from each present moment—that is, each moment when we are aware of the unfailing presence of God in our hearts.

Reflection

Take a little time today to be fully present to the present moment.

MARGARET SILF

The descent into the depths

Jesus said to her, 'Go, call your husband, and come back.' The woman answered him, 'I have no husband.' Jesus said to her, 'You are right in saying, "I have no husband"; for you have had five husbands, and the one you have now is not your husband. What you have said is true!' The woman said to him, 'Sir, I see that you are a prophet. Our ancestors worshipped on this mountain, but you say that the place where people must worship is in Jerusalem.'

There is a problem with wells. To reach the living water you first have to go down a deep, dark shaft and the journey to the bottom can be daunting indeed. We cannot see where we are going and have no idea what to expect when we arrive. Perhaps we fear a traumatic shock when we hit rock bottom.

It is easy to imagine the disappointment and maybe even dismay of the woman to whom Jesus has just promised living water that will quench her deepest thirst. He now appears to change the subject abruptly and steer her towards the topic she most dreads and least wants to talk about—her problems in personal relationships. Why does he do this? Why is it that when we try to follow the call of the one who leads us to the living water, we come up against those aspects of ourselves that we would rather not think about? Surely it is because for us, as for her, there is no way to reach the living water without descending to the depths of the well.

There is a lovely image of this encounter at the well by the Austrian artist Sieger Köder. It depicts a person gazing into the depths of the well, but seeing two faces gazing back up. The second face is that of Jesus. If we truly long for the living water that Jesus offers, we will, sooner or later, have to face the drop into the depths. We do not descend alone, however—we enter the darkness of the well hand in hand with Jesus.

Reflection

As you sit at the well with Jesus, what question might he ask you that would take you to the depths of your heart?

MARGARET SILF

From received faith to lived experience

Jesus said to her, 'Woman, believe me, the hour is coming when you will worship the Father neither on this mountain nor in Jerusalem. You worship what you do not know; we worship what we know, for salvation is from the Jews. But the hour is coming, and is now here, when true worshippers will worship the Father in spirit and in truth, for the Father seeks such as these to worship him. God is spirit, and those who worship him must worship in spirit and in truth.' The woman said to him, 'I know that Messiah is coming' (who is called Christ). 'When he comes, he will proclaim all things to us.' Jesus said to her, 'I am he, the one who is speaking to you.'

One of the woman's tactics for avoiding the searching question Jesus has put to her is to divert the conversation into a discussion about the correct location for worshipping God, but Jesus is not so easily distracted. The mystery in whom we live and move and have our being cannot be contained in a physical location, he tells her, just as the living water cannot be contained in a physical well.

When we speak of such questions we are way out of our depth. We are trying to use human logic to define a mystery that is, and always will be, far beyond the reach of our understanding. At the human level, the woman knows she will still come to the well every day for her water. What Jesus is opening up in her heart is the living water that will flood and transform the aching emptiness in the core of her being.

To have known the touch of God on our lives, however slightly and however rarely, is to be granted a knowledge that only the heart can grasp. The woman has been touched by Jesus in this way. She always knew, in her head, that the Messiah would come. Now received faith has been transformed into lived experience and nothing will ever be the same.

Reflection
Remember any moments in your life when you felt the touch of God.
How have they changed you?

MARGARET SILF

The water must flow

Just then his disciples came. They were astonished that he was speaking with a woman, but no one said, 'What do you want?' or, 'Why are you speaking with her?' Then the woman left her water-jar and went back to the city. She said to the people, 'Come and see a man who told me everything I have ever done! He cannot be the Messiah, can he?' They left the city and were on their way to him.

Jesus' encounter with the woman at the well has rendered his friends speechless. Their astonishment can be imagined only too clearly, given the hostility between Jews and Samaritans and the cultural taboo on speaking so freely with women, yet no one asks him what this is all about.

If I try to imagine myself being present at this scene, as one of Jesus' friends, I find myself asking, 'Why am I not plying him with questions?' Perhaps it is natural reticence. Perhaps it is the shock of finding one whom I revere in a potentially compromising situation. I think the most probable answer, however, is that, if I was there, I would probably have a growing awareness that this man walks to a different drumbeat and draws his authority from God, not from human traditions and customs.

The woman, however, has no such reservations. She returns to her village to tell everyone she meets about this remarkable man who could see right into her soul. She has felt the power of the encounter first hand. She has, we might say, drunk the water of life from the very source and experienced Jesus' power breaking into her life.

Now we see what happens to this living water that Jesus has released in her heart. Water is not static. It flows, inexorably, from its source in the heart of God, towards its destiny in the ocean of God's love and brings life to all it touches on the way.

The woman leaves her water jar behind in her haste to tell the whole village about Jesus. Her everyday concerns pale into insignificance in the new light that Jesus has ignited within her. The result? Everyone wants a taste of what she has. They set off to find Jesus for themselves.

Reflection

How much do our own lives reflect the fact that we have encountered Jesus?

MARGARET SILF

The bread of life

Meanwhile the disciples were urging him, 'Rabbi, eat something.' But he said to them, 'I have food to eat that you do not know about.' So the disciples said to one another, 'Surely no one has brought him something to eat?' Jesus said to them, 'My food is to do the will of him who sent me and to complete his work. Do you not say, "Four months more, then comes the harvest"? But I tell you, look around you, and see how the fields are ripe for harvesting. The reaper is already receiving wages and is gathering fruit for eternal life, so that the sower and reaper may rejoice together.'

Just as the woman was concerned with how to draw water without a bucket, so Jesus' friends continue to miss the point. They urge him to have something to eat, but he assures them that he has a source of nourishment of which they are unaware. He lives and thrives by being in right relationship with the source of his being. This bread of life that he brings to humanity is already growing and ready for harvest.

It is easy for us to see how the woman, disciples and others consistently miss the point of what Jesus is trying to teach them, but surely we would have missed the point, too? It is not an obvious leap, from well water to the water of life or from a picnic lunch to the bread of life. How should we understand Jesus' message here?

We began our reflections by recalling how birth begins with the waters breaking. Maybe that same image of a baby being born can help us understand better what Jesus is saying here. Just as an unborn child can have no grasp of the reality of life outside the womb, so we cannot imagine the power of the water and bread of life that Jesus brings. The nearest we can come is to start with the water in our wells and the bread on our tables. Jesus begins where we are and leads us towards truths deeper than anything we can imagine.

Reflection

We do not need to understand the power of the water and bread of life that Jesus offers. We only need to trust it.

MARGARET SILF

The water brings life to all

Many Samaritans from that city believed in him because of the woman's testimony, 'He told me everything I have ever done.' So when the Samaritans came to him, they asked him to stay with them; and he stayed there for two days. And many more believed because of his word. They said to the woman, 'It is no longer because of what you said that we believe, for we have heard for ourselves, and we know that this is truly the Saviour of the world.'

There comes a point in a journey of faith when it is no longer about what we have been told, but about what we have experienced. This is the point that the people of the Samaritan community have reached, following the woman's encounter with Jesus at the well.

It began with her testimony, though 'testimony' is rather a solemn word for what was more probably an exuberant outpouring of what had happened, an account flowing like a torrent from her super-charged heart. It began with her words, but the real energy of the moment surely lies in the obvious effects of what he said on her life.

We, too, can tell our stories of faith sedately and correctly, wondering that our listeners seem unmoved. Alternatively, we can reveal by the enthusiasm of our response something of the divine energy flowing through us as a result. No one will say to us, 'I want something of what you have' unless they see the effects of that 'something' in our lives.

We noticed earlier that, by definition, water flows. Jesus has released this flow in the Samaritan woman's heart, but she does not keep it to herself. She immediately goes to the town to share the good news. The result is that the people of the town flock to see Jesus for themselves and be touched by his power. Their knowledge has moved from head to heart, from second-hand account to first-hand experience. The water of life has fulfilled the purpose for which it was given—it has generated fresh and active spiritual life

Reflection

What has helped your faith to move from your head to your heart, from what you have been told to what you have experienced for yourself?

MARGARET SILF

Water transformed into wine

When the two days were over, he went from that place to Galilee (for Jesus himself had testified that a prophet has no honour in the prophet's own country). When he came to Galilee, the Galileans welcomed him, since they had seen all that he had done in Jerusalem at the festival; for they too had gone to the festival. Then he came again to Cana in Galilee where he had changed the water into wine.

During these past few days, we have seen how the water of life can break forth in our hearts to herald a spiritual new birth. We have also seen how it cleanses and purifies us and how it pours forth in our lives in ways that draw others to long for water from the same well. Today we see another aspect of that water of life—its ability to transform us.

After the encounter at the well, Jesus moves on to Galilee and, specifically, to the Galilean town of Cana, which is where he had performed his first miracle at a wedding feast (John 2:1–11). This had been a miracle of transformation *and* a miracle involving water. We recall how, on that occasion, when the hosts had run out of wine, Jesus had asked for the containers to be filled with water, but, when the stewards had drawn this water, it was found to be the finest wine.

Perhaps it is no accident that we are reminded of this miracle immediately following the release of the water of life in the heart of the Samaritan woman. When Jesus leads us to the water of life and sets free its flow in our lives, the effect is transformative. Our view of life and its meaning changes as surely as Jesus changed the water into wine at Cana—and not just any wine, but the very finest wine.

For the transformation to be effective, however, the wine needed to be poured out. Otherwise it might as well still have been water. In our lives, too, only in the pouring out—the living out—is the transformation made apparent.

Reflection

God has already changed the water of our everyday lives into the finest wine, but this transformation is only effective when we allow ourselves to be poured out for each other.

MARGARET SILF

19

From death to life

Now there was a royal official whose son lay ill in Capernaum. When he heard that Jesus had come from Judea to Galilee, he went and begged him to come down and heal his son, for he was at the point of death… The official said to him, 'Sir, come down before my little boy dies.' Jesus said to him, 'Go; your son will live.' The man believed the word that Jesus spoke to him and started on his way. As he was going down, his slaves met him and told him that his child was alive. So he asked them the hour when he began to recover, and they said to him, 'Yesterday at one in the afternoon the fever left him.' The father realised that this was the hour when Jesus had said to him, 'Your son will live.'

We began our reflections on the water of life with thoughts of new life, of being born or reborn. We conclude them with the greatest transformation of all—the coming back to life when close to death.

We have heard the questions of a curious but diffident Nicodemus faced with the challenge to be born again of the Spirit. Now we meet an official whose faith is such that he does not need to ask any questions, but trusts that Jesus' word alone will restore his son to life.

We have seen the life of a Samaritan woman turned upside down during a conversation with a passing stranger who asked her for a drink of water. Today, not life, but death is turned upside down as life is restored to a dying child.

We have been reminded that, in Jesus' hands, water can become the finest wine and here we discover that, with Jesus, death is transformed into life, not just for one family but also for the entire human family.

Our own journeys of faith may also begin with questions and failure to understand, but God meets us where we are and gently leads us deeper into the mystery, until we no longer rely on what we have been told, but learn to trust what we have experienced.

The water of life has done its work.

Prayer

Lord, give us your living water, that we may never thirst again.

MARGARET SILF

The Church

In the ups and downs of church life, it is often tempting to look back to earlier times, to some imagined 'golden age' supposedly free of the stresses and strains of the present day. However far back we look, I suspect that the Church has always experienced turbulence of one kind or another. Even the early days—the 'honeymoon' period—were not immune: a brief glance at the Acts of the Apostles and Paul's epistles to the Corinthians and Galatians make that abundantly clear!

The notes that follow begin with the ascension, which preceded Pentecost (24 May), but it was itself crucial to the beginnings of the Church. It was their witness of that event that first brought the male disciples of Jesus and some of his women followers—including his mother—together in prayer and fellowship. I have prefaced several of the notes with phrases from the hymn 'The Church's one foundation', using them as springboards for our exploration of some of the different aspects of the Church's life—past, present and future.

We will see in the notes how Jesus Christ, as the 'one foundation' of the Church, serves as both encourager (15 May) and rebuker regarding those things that continue to separate us (21 May). We explore, with Paul, something of what it means to be 'members of one body' (18 May). 'Partakes one holy food' (20 May) looks at Holy Communion and 'By water and the Word' (17 May) considers the Church's sacrament of baptism, together with another, largely forgotten, water ceremony initiated by Jesus: washing the disciples' feet.

Fellowship may be the lifeblood of our churches, but we also consider those whose vocations are different. 'In the wilderness' begins with the early desert ministry of John the Baptist, then considers the role of those who have been called to contemplative—sometimes solitary—prayer.

In 'Saints their watch are keeping', we remind ourselves that the Church exists both vertically through time and horizontally in the present and we are part of a continuity which extends from the distant past and onwards into the unimaginable future. Wherever we are on the timeline, however, the aim and focus are the same: 'the vision glorious' and the time when God will bring all things to their final completion in Christ.

Barbara Mosse

Out of their sight

[The apostles] asked him, 'Lord, is this the time when you will restore the kingdom to Israel?' He replied, 'It is not for you to know the times or the periods that the Father has set... But you will receive power when the Holy Spirit has come upon you; and you will be my witnesses in Jerusalem, in all Judea and Samaria, and to the ends of the earth.' When he had said this, as they were watching, he was lifted up, and a cloud took him out of their sight... Then they returned to Jerusalem... [and] were constantly devoting themselves to prayer, together with certain women, including Mary the mother of Jesus, as well as his brothers.

The feast of Pentecost, which will be the focus of our reflection on 24 May, is traditionally celebrated as the birthday of the Church. Arguably, however, it is with today's festival of the ascension that the seeds of the infant church began to grow.

How is it possible for us to visualise the ascension? Artists through-out the ages have struggled to depict the event, sometimes with quite comical results. When anyone has attempted to use words, it is a matter of trying to describe the indescribable. Of the Gospel writers, only Luke attempts it and he has left us two versions: the account offered in today's passage from Acts and a variant reading towards the end of his Gospel (Luke 24:44–47, 50–51).

The initial gathering was modest in number, comprising the eleven apostles who remained after Judas' treachery (Acts 1:13), Jesus' brothers and 'certain women, including Mary the mother of Jesus' (1:14). What was the first action of this fledgling community? Luke makes it clear that their priority was prayer, to which they devoted themselves constantly. In the church today, surely there can be no greater priority for us either as together we seek the mind and will of God, who prompts and nudges us from the depths of his divine love.

Reflection

'You have heard; now see all this; and will you not declare it? From this time forward I make you hear new things, hidden things that you have not known' (Isaiah 48:6).

BARBARA MOSSE

The Church's one foundation

He is the image of the invisible God, the firstborn of all creation; for in him all things in heaven and on earth were created, things visible and invisible... all things have been created through him and for him. He himself is before all things, and in him all things hold together. He is the head of the body, the church; he is the beginning, the firstborn from the dead... For in him all the fullness of God was pleased to dwell, and through him God was pleased to reconcile to himself all things, whether on earth or in heaven, by making peace through the blood of his cross.

'The Church's one foundation is Jesus Christ her Lord.' So opens the traditional hymn, concisely summing up the beliefs expressed in today's passage. The detail in this passage from Colossians—the so-called 'Colossian hymn'—certainly bears close attention. Its scope is cosmic and its thoughts bear striking parallels with those expressed in John 1:1–14. So Christ is 'before all things' (Colossians 1:17) and 'in the beginning with God' (John 1:2). 'All things have been created through him and for him' (Colossians 1:16) and 'All things came into being through him' (John 1:3). 'In him all the fullness of God was pleased to dwell' (Colossians 1:19) and 'the Word was God' (John 1:1).

If we ponder the words of the passage from Colossians, our limited viewpoints will inevitably be challenged and we will see the Church from a fresh perspective. It is all too easy for the church today, fragmented into a multitude of different denominations, to lose sight of its essential unity in Christ. The church is also depressingly liable to 'take its eye off the ball' and become bogged down in the politics and minutiae of its institutional life. The words of the Colossian hymn invite us to shake off our earth-bound ways and lift our eyes to the heavens, to our Father God who established his Son as head of the Church and through whom we and all things were created.

Reflection

'So then you are... members of the household of God, built upon the foundation of the apostles and prophets, with Christ Jesus himself as the cornerstone' (Ephesians 2:19–20).

Barbara Mosse

Fellowship with God—and one another

> If we say that we have fellowship with [God] while we are walking
> in darkness, we lie and do not do what is true; but if we walk in
> the light as he himself is in the light, we have fellowship with one
> another, and the blood of Jesus his Son cleanses us from all sin…
> If we confess our sins, he who is faithful and just will forgive us
> our sins and cleanse us from all unrighteousness.

I once attended a church where an elderly woman in the congregation
refused to receive the chalice from another, younger woman, a lay assis-
tant in the parish. The reasons for the older woman's taking offence
were almost lost in the mists of time, but apparently had something to
do with a misunderstanding over the baking of cakes for a church function. The younger woman was unaware of what exactly she was supposed to have done wrong, but had made repeated attempts to heal the
breach. She was rebuffed every time. The rift was causing upset within
the wider congregation and the minister was urged to sit down with the
two women and try to help them towards reconciliation. He refused to
do so, afraid that the older woman would stop coming to services if
confronted, so her hostility and her visibly broken relationship with the
younger woman continued to undermine the sacrament and spread like
a cancer through the fellowship.

In our worst moments, we may find it far easier to nurse a grudge
than let it go and freely forgive. There are times when forgiveness has to
be a process, rather than an instant act; times when the desire to be able
to forgive is all we can manage at that point. Our sense of justice has
been outraged and we cry out for recompense or at least an apology,
which may or may not be forthcoming. So, the teaching in today's passage is hard, but it is vital for the healthy life and growth of our church
fellowships.

Reflection

*How 'open' is your church fellowship? Is there an atmosphere of security
and trust? Are the inevitable disagreements that arise in any groups of
people able to be brought to Christ for healing and forgiveness?*

BARBARA MOSSE

MATTHEW 28:16–20 (NRSV)

By water and the word

Now the eleven disciples went to Galilee, to the mountain to which Jesus had directed them. When they saw him, they worshipped him; but some doubted. And Jesus came and said to them, 'All authority in heaven and on earth has been given to me. Go therefore and make disciples of all nations, baptising them in the name of the Father and of the Son and of the Holy Spirit, and teaching them to obey everything that I have commanded you. And remember, I am with you always, to the end of the age.'

'She is his new creation by water and the word.' Thus continues our hymn as it begins to explore more deeply the Church whose 'one foundation' is Jesus Christ.

Today's passage is the closing words to Matthew's Gospel, which are more usually associated with Trinity Sunday. The passage includes the familiar words used at baptism, mentioning all three persons of the Trinity (28:19); however, its interest for us lies not in a deep trinitarian discussion but in its association of water (baptism) and word (teaching).

This association was not unique to the Church. Our early introduction to John the Baptist sees him combining baptism with a call to repentance (Luke 3:3), an act whose intention would be 'proved' by the believer's subsequent change of life (vv. 10–14). Over the centuries, baptism became the authenticating mark of church membership.

Scripture tells us of another water initiation ceremony—one instigated by Jesus himself. John 13 relates how, on the evening before his death, Jesus washed his disciples' feet. Peter's resistance was met with the bluntest possible challenge (v. 8) and Jesus' subsequent words pressed the point home: 'You also ought to wash one another's feet. For I have set you an example, that you also should do as I have done to you' (vv. 14–15). Despite Jesus' insistence on the ritual's continuing importance, however, the church has generally chosen not to act on his words. Why might that be, I wonder?

Reflection

'Peter said to him, "You will never wash my feet." Jesus answered, "Unless I wash you, you have no share with me"' (John 13:8).

BARBARA MOSSE

Members of one body

Now there are varieties of gifts, but the same Spirit; and there are varieties of services... but it is the same God who activates all of them in everyone. To each is given the manifestation of the Spirit for the common good... For just as the body is one and has many members, and all the members of the body, though many, are one body, so it is with Christ. For in the one Spirit we were all baptised into one body—Jews or Greeks, slaves or free... God has so arranged the body... that there may be no dissension within the body, but the members may have the same care for one another. If one member suffers, all suffer together with it; if one member is honoured, all rejoice together with it.

Paul's aspirational descriptions of the Church as a perfectly working body may cause a wry smile when we recall some of the less worthy, grittier aspects of its institutional life. How unlike a perfectly functioning body we feel most of the time! Paul, however, reminds us of our essential unity and the fact that this is the spiritual reality, regardless of our personal experience seeming to diverge from it.

By using his picture of a perfectly functioning body, Paul highlights various areas of importance. First, we are all different and the gifts we are given will also differ. In my experience, quite a bit of friction at local church level arises from a lack of recognition that we are not all called to work for God in the exactly the same way. I think of it as the 'Martha' principle: 'I am on the coffee rota—why isn't she?' One of the greatest gifts to have come out of the Fresh Expressions movement is the realisation of the enormous variety of ways in which people can be encouraged along Christ's path, whether that be via a church set up in a coffee shop or pub or initiatives such as Messy Church.

Most importantly, Paul offers a timely reminder that we are not Christians in isolation. Anything that happens to one member of the body inevitably affects all the others, whether for good or ill.

Reflection

'We are members of one another' (Ephesians 4:25).

Barbara Mosse

Saints their watch are keeping

There was also a prophet, Anna the daughter of Phanuel, of the tribe of Asher. She was of a great age, having lived with her husband for seven years after her marriage, then as a widow to the age of eighty-four. She never left the temple but worshipped there with fasting and prayer night and day. At that moment she came, and began to praise God and to speak about the child to all who were looking for the redemption of Jerusalem.

Yesterday's Bible passage anchored us in our 'horizontal' experience of the present-day church. Today's, with the above title taken from our hymn, reminds us of the 'vertical' dimension of the church, as we seek to travel and watch in communion with saints past and present.

The reading introduces us to one such saint: 'Anna the daughter of Phanuel' (Luke 2:36). She is a woman of great age, whose calling at this late stage of her life is as a contemplative (v. 37). With Anna, Luke challenges today's church in two particular areas: its attitude to its elderly and its experience—or lack of experience—of contemplative prayer.

Regarding the elderly, it is not unusual to hear of churches that tolerate a contemplative prayer ministry in those who, whether because of age or illness, are no longer able to exercise an 'active' ministry (or 'useful' ministry, as the unspoken meaning). For those who are tempted to diminish the role of both contemplative prayer and the elderly in this way, it should be noted that Luke's Anna was not only a contemplative but also an evangelist (v. 38).

Regarding contemplative prayer, it is clearly not only the old who are called to this ministry. Mary of Bethany, sitting at the feet of Jesus, was clearly a contemplative and, as such, was severely judged by her sister Martha (Luke 10:38–42). Today's younger contemplatives may also find understanding within their church communities hard to come by, for much the same reasons Martha offered. Such communities should note Jesus' response to Martha!

Prayer

'For God alone my soul waits in silence; from him comes my salvation'
(Psalm 62:1).

BARBARA MOSSE

Partakes one holy food

> Jesus said, 'I am the bread of life. Whoever comes to me will never be hungry, and whoever believes in me will never be thirsty... I am the living bread that came down from heaven. Whoever eats of this bread will live for ever; and the bread that I will give for the life of the world is my flesh.'

Today, our hymn moves on to a key element in the life of the Church: the partaking of 'one holy food'. Whether known as Holy Communion, the Mass, the Agape, the Eucharist or the Lord's Supper, the community's sharing of the bread and the wine in commemoration of/participation in Jesus' sacrifice on the cross has become the expression of our membership of Christ's body, the Church. A continuing scandal lies in our awareness that this focus of unity has, through the centuries, become one of the most significant flashpoints of our disunity. When we consider the open-hearted invitation implied in Jesus' words in this passage, the church's ongoing differences can only be a cause of continuing pain and regret.

We know only too well that there is no immediate magic wand that can solve our institutional differences, but today's passage from John's Gospel encourages us to take a higher and broader view. Jesus' words carry a flavour of the Gospel prologue's cosmic tone: 'Whoever eats of this bread will live for ever; and the bread that I will give for the life of the world is my flesh' (John 6:51). These words form part of a much longer passage (vv. 35–59) in which Jesus reminds the people of that time when God fed their ancestors with manna in the wilderness. Then, God sustained his own chosen people; now, through the life and death of Jesus, the range of God's provision is infinitely extended: '*Whoever eats of this bread will live for ever; and the bread that I will give for the life of the world is my flesh*' (emphasis added).

Prayer

Lord, you are the bread of life. Forgive the church the damage she has inflicted on your gift of love and make us increasingly open to a healing of our divisions. Amen

BARBARA MOSSE

By schisms rent asunder

And so, brothers and sisters, I could not speak to you as spiritual people, but rather as people of the flesh, as infants in Christ. I fed you with milk, not solid food; for you were not ready for solid food. Even now you are still not ready, for you are still of the flesh. For as long as there is jealousy and quarrelling among you, are you not of the flesh, and behaving according to human inclinations? For when one says, 'I belong to Paul', and another, 'I belong to Apollos', are you not merely human?

Yesterday, we considered something of the damage caused to the church by its denominational divisions, with the Eucharist as a continuing, visible focus of that disunity. Sadly, the history of the church demonstrates that this is nothing new. Samuel J. Stone, writing our hymn during the turbulent 19th century, described the church of his era as being 'by schisms rent asunder', and today's passage from 1 Corinthians makes it clear that, even in those halcyon early days, the church of Paul's time was not immune either.

Paul's frustration with the Corinthians leaps off the page: the phrase 'tearing his hair out' comes to mind! Like babies who must be fed on milk, the people are still not ready for 'solid food'. Why? Because of the 'jealousy and quarrelling' (v. 3) that is rife in the community and the people's distressing tendency to split into factions at the first opportunity: '"I belong to Paul"… "I belong to Apollos"' (v. 4).

Life situations may change but human nature does not, and both the problems highlighted by Paul are readily recognisable within our local church life. A poisonous situation can be created in a church where one minister is preferred over another, perhaps because their respective gifts (preaching and pastoral work, for example) are unequally valued. As for 'jealousy and quarrelling', they continue to wreak havoc now, as then.

Reflection

'Now I appeal to you, brothers and sisters, by the name of our Lord Jesus Christ, that all of you should be in agreement and that there should be no divisions among you, but that you should be united in the same mind and the same purpose' (1 Corinthians 1:10).

Barbara Mosse

For her life he died

> [Jesus said] 'I am the good shepherd. The good shepherd lays down his life for the sheep... I know my own and my own know me, just as the Father knows me and I know the Father. And I lay down my life for the sheep. I have other sheep that do not belong to this fold. I must bring them also, and they will listen to my voice. So there will be one flock, one shepherd. For this reason the Father loves me, because I lay down my life in order to take it up again. No one takes it from me, but I lay it down of my own accord.'

Today's line from our hymn in the title above highlights the theme of the passage: Christ's voluntary laying down of his life for the life of his people. In the imagery of the hymn, this self-sacrifice is for the Church, Christ's 'holy bride', but in the passage from John's Gospel, he picks up and develops the image of the shepherd and his sheep.

There was nothing new or unusual about this imagery. In probably the most familiar Davidic psalm in the Old Testament, it is God—the Lord—who is the shepherd, who 'makes me lie down in green pastures' and 'restores my soul' (Psalm 23:2–3). God here, as shepherd, accompanies the believer through life, comforting, shielding from harm, protecting from evil (vv. 4–6). In Ezekiel 34:11–16, God is the true shepherd of Israel who unleashes his anger on those false shepherds who feed themselves rather than their sheep and fail to offer them protection (vv. 1–6).

In our passage from John's Gospel, Jesus proclaims himself as the 'good shepherd' (John 10:1) who gives his life for his sheep, but further develops the idea in the direction of unity. He is quite clear that the laying down of the shepherd's life is not only for the individual or even just for the Israelite nation but also for the 'other sheep that do not belong to this fold' (v. 16).

Reflection

'So there will be one flock, one shepherd' (v. 16). How open is the church today to those 'not of this fold', whether Christian or not? How big a problem is insularity for the church?

BARBARA MOSSE

In the wilderness

Now the time came for Elizabeth to give birth, and she bore a son... The child grew and became strong in spirit, and he was in the wilderness until the day he appeared publicly to Israel.

It is intriguing to find that, while all commentaries address the verse about John's birth (v. 57), very few consider the one concerning his being 'in the wilderness' (v. 80). Perhaps this is in part because of the ongoing difficulty that our often over-busy church has with the idea of withdrawal from the world. In addition to John the Baptist, there are numerous examples of withdrawal in both the Old and New Testaments. Among these are Elijah's significant encounter with God in the wilderness in 1 Kings 19:1–18 and the Israelites' 40-year period of preparation and spiritual growth during their wilderness wanderings in the book of Exodus (chapter 12 and onwards). In the New Testament, both Jesus (Matthew 4:1–11) and Paul (Galatians 1:16–17) also withdrew for periods of time before beginning their public ministries.

The medieval church was not so resistant. Most towns and villages would have had a resident hermit, authorised by the bishop and following a daily cycle of prayer. The hermit would often contribute to the life of the community through activities such as road mending and bridge building. Similarly, anchorites and anchoresses (most famously, perhaps, Julian of Norwich) were people whose lives were given over to prayer. Their cells were often literally 'anchored' to the wall of their local parish church, where people could visit them for spiritual guidance.

Although such vocations, both solitary and communal, do exist in today's church, they tend to be more hidden. Robustly challenging this tendency, the Archbishop of Canterbury, Justin Welby, recently established a small ecumenical religious community at Lambeth Palace. He stated that the decline of such communities, dedicated to prayer, is 'an alarm call' to the whole church, and that without the flourishing of such communities there can be no renewal.

Reflection

'Now during those days [Jesus] went out to the mountain to pray; and he spent the night in prayer to God' (Luke 6:12).

BARBARA MOSSE

Receive the Holy Spirit

When it was evening on that day, the first day of the week, and the doors of the house where the disciples had met were locked for fear of the Jews, Jesus came and stood among them and said, 'Peace be with you.' After he said this, he showed them his hands and his side. Then the disciples rejoiced when they saw the Lord. Jesus said to them again, 'Peace be with you. As the Father has sent me, so I send you.' When he had said this, he breathed on them and said to them, 'Receive the Holy Spirit. If you forgive the sins of any, they are forgiven them; if you retain the sins of any, they are retained.'

Commenting on this passage, the scholar Gail O'Day observes that 'most Protestant Christians are not well attuned to Easter as a liturgical season; after Easter Sunday, Protestant church expectations return to something like business as usual' (*Feasting on the Word: Year B, Volume 2*, p. 401). She goes on to say that the Easter season continues for a full seven weeks, culminating in the feast of Pentecost celebrating the coming of the Holy Spirit.

Today's passage from John's Gospel offers us the quieter and more private counterpart to the very dramatic and public coming of the Spirit described in Acts 2:1–13. It takes place during one of Christ's resurrection appearances to his disciples and Jesus breathes the Spirit on them, conveying his peace and the commission to minister in his name.

The verse about forgiving and retaining sins is complex and has given rise to much theological controversy, but John's particular understanding of sin is important here. In this Gospel, sin is seen more as a refusal to see the truth than a lapse in behaviour or morals (which is the emphasis in Matthew 18:18). For John, to have sin is to be blind to the revelation of God in Jesus Christ (John 9:41). Elsewhere, the Gospel states that part of the Spirit's role is to 'prove the world wrong about sin' (16:8) and in today's passage Christ makes clear that the Christian community is to continue this work.

Prayer

Breathe on me, breath of God; fill me with life anew.

Edwin Hatch, 1878

BARBARA MOSSE

The infant church

Awe came upon everyone, because many wonders and signs were being done by the apostles. All who believed were together and had all things in common; they would sell their possessions and goods and distribute the proceeds to all, as any had need. Day by day, as they spent much time together in the temple, they broke bread at home and ate their food with glad and generous hearts, praising God and having the goodwill of all the people. And day by day the Lord added to their number those who were being saved.

Much of Jesus' teaching during his public ministry indicated that God's ways represent a dramatic reversal of the normal ways of the world. He taught that the first shall be last and the last, first (Mark 10:31), the one who wishes to save their life must lose it (Luke 9:24) and it is the meek who will inherit the earth (Matthew 5:5). This teaching built on earlier prophecies that spoke of a time when the wolf and the lamb shall feed together (Isaiah 65:25) and death itself would be destroyed (Isaiah 25:8).

In today's passage from Acts, we see the signs of this divine reversal beginning to take place in the fledgling church—a reversal that has only become possible since Jesus' resurrection and the coming of the Spirit at Pentecost. The picture Luke paints is of a community birthed in awe and wonder and in humble gratitude for the gifts God has poured on them through Christ. Such thankful awareness cannot help but give of itself in the welcome and service of others. The people's joy is infectious and, through their open-hearted generosity, the kingdom begins to deepen its roots.

We see welcome glimpses of this reality, but much of the day-to-day experience of our institutional churches can seem light years away from it. The challenge to us today—as it has been to believers in every age—is to allow our roots to be deepened, beyond the point where sin and superficial difficulties are able to disturb them.

Reflection

In what ways may we, both as individuals and local church fellowships, more effectively experience and express the eternal values of God's kingdom?

BARBARA MOSSE

Mystic sweet communion

Therefore, since we are surrounded by so great a cloud of witnesses, let us also lay aside every weight and the sin that clings so closely, and let us run with perseverance the race that is set before us, looking to Jesus the pioneer and perfecter of our faith, who for the sake of the joy that was set before him endured the cross, disregarding its shame, and has taken his seat at the right hand of the throne of God.

The title taken from our hymn today reminds us of the church's 'mystic sweet communion with those whose rest is won'. Whatever the triumphs and disasters of the church in our own time, these words, and the words of today's passage from Hebrews, remind us that we are members of the Church of Christ, which is rooted in eternity. As noted previously, our fellowship within the church has a vertical as well as a horizontal dimension and the writer to the Hebrews reminds his readers of the 'cloud of witnesses' that surrounds them as they undertake their own Christian journey (Hebrews 11 details these Old Testament heroes of faith, both named and unnamed).

If we are prepared to consciously enter into this eternal dimension, our awareness of those who have gone before us can offer real encouragement. We may, for example, read the words of Julian of Norwich, Thomas Merton or St John of the Cross and experience their words communicating directly with us across the chasm between their time and our own. It is as if they are speaking to us directly and this creates a sense of real kinship, however wide the distance is in terms of geography and time. However different their circumstances were from our own, we sense that we are sharing a common journey.

As the writer to the Hebrews reminds us, the focus of all our journeys, in whatever age, is 'Jesus, the pioneer and perfecter of our faith' (12:2) and he is the reason that it is possible to 'run with perseverance the race that is set before us' (v. 1).

Reflection

We are members of a church that has a vertical as well as a horizontal dimension. How does this reality impact your own spiritual journey?

BARBARA MOSSE

The vision glorious

Then I saw a new heaven and a new earth; for the first heaven and the first earth had passed away… And I saw the holy city, the new Jerusalem, coming down out of heaven from God, prepared as a bride adorned for her husband. And I heard a loud voice from the throne saying, 'See, the home of God is among mortals. He will dwell with them; they will be his peoples…' I saw no temple in the city, for its temple is the Lord God the Almighty and the Lamb. And the city has no need of sun or moon to shine on it, for the glory of God is its light, and its lamp is the Lamb.

The penultimate verse of our hymn takes up all the images concerning the Church that it has explored and directs our thoughts towards 'the vision glorious' to which all those images point. That vision is expanded more fully in today's passage from Revelation, with its description of 'a new heaven and a new earth' (v. 1). The text describes not the Church, but the new Jerusalem as 'a bride adorned for her husband' (v. 2). With the promise that 'the home of God is among mortals' (v. 3), the writer projects us forwards to the consummation of all history when all things are finally gathered up in and under God.

Here, surely, lies our hope during those times when we feel either bogged down by the present difficulties of the church or in near despair over its sometimes shameful past. It lies in the fact that scripture makes clear, whatever humanity, throughout history, makes of it, the role of the visible, institutional church is not the final reality. The vision the writer of Revelation saw was that there was 'no temple in the city, for its temple is the Lord God the Almighty and the Lamb' (21:22). The function of the church, then, is transitory. Whatever our present experience may be, the visionary encourages us to keep our inner eyes on this truth. If we are able to do this, then the triumphs and disasters of the church in every time and place are put in their true perspective and receive ultimate healing in God.

Prayer

'Amen. Come Lord Jesus!' (Revelation 22:20).

BARBARA MOSSE

Significant women of the scriptures

In preparation for writing these pieces, I asked a large number of women about their favourite female characters in the biblical narratives. They gave me far too much material to fit into ten short notes!

Much of what you will find here comes from the choices, insights and reflections of those women, who are ministers and theologians, scholars and preachers. There is not space to acknowledge them individually, but I pay tribute to them and their lives, which are as varied, exciting and rich in God's gifts as the 'significant women of the scriptures' whom they admire. Of course I have drawn on the wisdom of male scholars, too, for it is surely when our insights are combined that we learn and gain the most.

We cannot escape the fact that the Hebrew and Christian scriptures (or the Old and New Testaments), although formed and shaped over centuries and in many different communities and contexts, are written primarily from a patriarchal standpoint. The majority of the biblical material is by and about men. What we learn about the women of the scriptures has to be carefully sought out and examined, then interpreted by means of the historic and biblical scholarship that are such gifts to our understanding of the texts and the contexts in which they were written.

Having spent several months living with these biblical women, and others whose stories I have had to leave untold, I am overwhelmed by the abundance of what they have to teach us. They respond to God's touch in their lives in ways that challenge, inform and inspire: relishing God's creation, learning to be wily and tenacious, leading by resistance, being admirable pioneers, shaming the powerful, filling their boots when the moment demanded, taking risks and staying with the consequences, showing us God's intimacy, standing tall in the resurrection and putting all their resources into the proclamation of the gospel.

Often in spite of rather than because of their circumstances, these women were leaders and protesters, change activists, apostles and spiritual pioneers. They lived out God's purposes with ingenuity and wisdom. They were courageous and intuitive. They have so much to teach us.

I pray that the lives of these women will enrich yours as much as they have inspired mine.

Rosemary Lain-Priestley

Eve

Then God said, 'Let us make humankind in our image, according to our likeness…' So God created humankind in his image, in the image of God he created them; male and female he created them.

A series about women in the scriptures has to begin with Eve. Her legacy is too significant to ignore and, in its popular version, too damaging to women to be left unchallenged. The most common understanding of the creation story is that Eve was made as Adam's subordinate and, by implication, his inferior, and her weakness became the portal through which evil entered the world. There is, however, a different interpretation that, although disputed by some theologians, has literary and biblical credibility. It also resonates more faithfully with the rich ways in which women have experienced God throughout Jewish and Christian history.

This other version says that, in God's image, an earth creature was formed who had no specific gender identity and only when woman was created were male and female made distinct. Eve was built not from a single rib, but from one of Adam's 'sides'. Adam recognised in her his co-responding partner, they both fully possessed the potential to reflect God's image and they were equally culpable for the loss of paradise.

What, though, was their sin exactly? Was it sheer disobedience and misplaced ambition or something more complex and subtle? Whatever it was, it is something that we have inherited, which is the point of the story. Most likely, it was their failure to draw the line between a passionate and protective engagement with the gift of creation and the greed that grasps, controls and abuses the gift.

Eve's legacy to us is also Adam's and it is a potent mix: our thoughtless misuse of life's good gifts alongside our tremendous capacity to nurture and connect with the divine in every detail of creation. Equally made in God's image, we are equally redeemed. Knowing this, we share the task to love and nurture the garden.

Prayer

God of grace, you have created all your children in your image. As the beauty of the world reflects your glory, may my life, too, speak of your abundance and love. Amen

ROSEMARY LAIN-PRIESTLEY

Sarah and Hagar

The angel of the Lord found [Hagar] by a spring of water in the wilderness, the spring on the way to Shur. And he said, 'Hagar, slave-girl of Sarai, where have you come from and where are you going?' She said, 'I am running away from my mistress Sarai.' The angel of the Lord said to her, 'Return to your mistress, and submit to her.'

In Genesis 12:2, Abram receives a promise that God will make of him a great nation. Not, however, without the help of a woman or, as it turns out, two women. Abram's wife Sarai focuses all her resources on the fulfilment of God's promise. Finding that she cannot conceive, in accordance with tradition, she offers Abram her slave, Hagar. On the one hand, this saves face for Sarai, but, on the other, it also causes her much anguish.

Unable to contain her jealousy after Ishmael is born, Sarai ill-treats Hagar, who attempts to run away. Hagar's route towards her home country of Egypt is through the wilderness—a place of encounter with God. There, Hagar meets the angel of the Lord, who tells her to return to her mistress. In a remarkable exchange, this woman—a slave far from home and in danger—summons dignity and courage and enters into a dialogue with God. The first person in the Bible to do so, she names God as, 'The God of seeing' or 'God who sees me' (16:13).

Hagar returns to her mistress and their complicated relationship, with its potent mix of fertility and infertility, power and powerlessness. With the surprise birth of Isaac, which means 'laughter', to Sarai, renamed Sarah, in her old age, the pressure is too much for everyone. Hagar is ejected and once more encounters God in the desert, this time being given a new life and a future for herself and Ishmael (21:8–21).

These tenacious, stubborn, sometimes unkind, but always resourceful, women are God's partners in delivering the divine purposes. God sees them both, knows their strengths and faults and, in different ways, honours them. The promise is fulfilled, if somewhat messily.

Reflection

Think about those people you find difficult. What can you learn from them? Is there any way in which they can even 'name God' for you?

ROSEMARY LAIN-PRIESTLEY

Shiphrah and Puah

The king of Egypt said to the Hebrew midwives, one of whom was named Shiphrah and the other Puah, 'When you act as midwives to the Hebrew women, and see them on the birthstool, if it is a boy, kill him; but if it is a girl, she shall live.' But the midwives feared God; they did not do as the king of Egypt commanded them, but they let the boys live.

This story takes place when the Hebrews are in captivity in Egypt and a source of forced labour. For reasons that are not obvious, Pharaoh decides to launch a system of population control among them, aiming to stop the flow of male children. He summons two midwives, Shiphrah and Puah. They listen politely to his orders, then go away and simply ignore them. In doing so, they take a huge risk. Pharaoh could easily have killed them for their disobedience.

The key to the midwives' actions, or inaction, is that, although they fear Pharaoh, they actually fear God more. Put more positively, they know that Pharaoh's power is relative and God's is absolute. Their loyalty is to God and their survival depends on God, not Pharaoh.

Shiphrah and Puah understand that they are part of a bigger picture, a picture that Pharaoh with his limited perspective does not see. From this they draw the courage to disobey. Their power is subversive, because they act by refusing to do something. In their story, we see the potency of a quiet refusal to conform. They even retain a sense of humour during the course of these fraught events, telling Pharaoh that the Hebrew women give birth more quickly than the Egyptians and they simply cannot get there in time.

It is easy to be persuaded or misled sometimes by those who have authority over us. If we are asked to do something that we believe goes against God's purposes, we might remind ourselves who it is really inspires awe and wonder in our lives.

Prayer

Lord, when I am tempted to capitulate to those in authority despite the fact that their actions are wrong, remind me of Shiphrah and Puah. Give me humour, ingenuity and the courage to stand my ground. Amen

ROSEMARY LAIN-PRIESTLEY

Leah and Rachel

But in the evening [Laban] took his daughter Leah and brought her to Jacob; and he went in to her... When morning came, it was Leah! And Jacob said to Laban, 'What is this you have done to me? Did I not serve with you for Rachel?...' Then Laban gave him his daughter Rachel as a wife... So Jacob went in to Rachel also, and he loved Rachel more than Leah.

Laban did not want to break tradition and allow Rachel to marry before her elder sister, so he deceived Jacob into marrying Leah first. This one decision, possibly well meant, set the stage for his daughters' misery. Jacob and Leah have many children, but he never comes to love her. Rachel is very much loved by Jacob, but they are unable to have children together. Had they found a way to comfort and sustain one another, the sisters' lives might have had a very different colour and texture. Instead, they allow their separate griefs to estrange them from one another.

It is sometimes said that 'not all women are sisters'. Just because people are in the same boat, they will not necessarily support one another. Unfortunately, in Rachel and Leah we see that not all sisters are sisters either. We should not judge them too harshly. We all have a tendency to be self-absorbed sometimes, finding it difficult to see beyond our own situation in order to empathise with others—and their situation was pretty dire.

Eventually Jacob, Leah and Rachel do collaborate in order to escape Laban's influence and control. There is a wonderfully rebellious part of the story when Rachel steals her father's household gods and sits on them (a more literal translation suggests that actually she menstruates on them, 31:33–35)! In rebelling against their father, did the sisters ultimately find comfort in one another? The story as we have it does not answer that question, but we might allow ourselves to hope they did.

Prayer

Lord, help me to see others as sisters and brothers, not rivals for life's good gifts. May I see past my own desires to the needs of other people. May we find in one another the fertile ground for friendship and peace. Amen

ROSEMARY LAIN-PRIESTLEY

Deborah the prophetess

At that time Deborah, a prophetess, wife of Lappidoth, was judging
Israel… She sent and summoned Barak son of Abinoam… and said
to him, 'The Lord, the God of Israel, commands you, "Go, take position at Mount Tabor… I will draw out Sisera… and I will give him
into your hand."' Barak said to her, 'If you will go with me, I will go.'

Deborah appears without preamble in the pages of the Hebrew scriptures. She is an unexpected feminine presence, the fourth of Israel's
judges and the only woman to have fulfilled that role.

When we meet her on this occasion, she is setting out the battle plan
that will ensure the defeat of Sisera, an enemy of her people who has
900 iron chariots at his disposal. Barak does not question Deborah's
leadership or judgement. He asks her to accompany him on the mission, which he does perhaps because he feels that this will increase his
chances of survival. We are given no privileged insight into Deborah's
mind, but we get the impression of a woman with considerable knowledge, wisdom and skill, who calmly faces the task set before her and
efficiently takes it in hand.

Deborah's leadership was exercised within the social constraints of
her time. As a woman, she could not appropriately hold court under her
own roof, so she sat 'under the palm of Deborah… and the Israelites
came up to her for judgement' (v. 5). She has been praised for her
impressive gravitas as a female leader in a male world and, conversely,
criticised for a leadership style that is stereotypically male. Female leaders of today are in good company!

Whether we are pioneers because of our gender, ethnicity, sexuality,
age or social background, being 'the first' carries considerable challenges. We are swept up in other people's expectations and projections
and have to face our own insecurities. In all of this, may we, like
Deborah, find ways in which we can feel comfortable in our own skin.

Reflection

*You are called to be yourself, not someone else. Each of us reflects God
uniquely in the world. Remember this, as you learn to be more fully and
more comfortably the person God has created you to be.*

ROSEMARY LAIN-PRIESTLEY

Esther

> Mordecai told them to reply to Esther, 'Do not think that in the king's palace you will escape any more than all the other Jews. For if you keep silence at such a time as this, relief and deliverance will rise for the Jews from another quarter, but you and your father's family will perish. Who knows? Perhaps you have come to royal dignity for just such a time as this.'

Esther is an orphaned Jewish woman living in Persia, brought up by her cousin, Mordecai. When she is recruited to the harem of King Ahasuerus and crowned queen, she keeps her Jewish identity secret. Then the lives of the Jews come under threat and Mordecai sends a message to Esther asking her to plead with the king to save them.

Prevaricating, Esther explains that, if she enters the king's presence without being invited, she will be put to death, unless he holds out his sceptre to her. Mordecai replies, essentially, 'Only you can do this and there are a lot of people relying on you to do it. If you do not, we will survive somehow, but you might not. This is your moment.'

This is a story about responsibility and calling. There is also a principle here that, if we recognise it, holds us to account. We all have our equivalent of Esther's 'royal dignity', which is whatever we have been given that can be used to change the world for the better. We often need one another's support in fulfilling that dignity, such as, crucially, when Esther asks Mordecai to organise a fast to strengthen her courage and he does it (4:15–17).

In the event, the king holds out his life-saving sceptre (5:2), Esther makes her plea and the Jewish people are saved. Esther needed that challenge from Mordecai in order to find the focus and the courage to act. She had to be reminded of her 'royal dignity'. That is something we must do for one another and even, sometimes, for ourselves.

Reflection

Is God asking you to act to change something for the better? How might Esther's story inspire you to take up your 'royal dignity'? Is there someone you know who needs to be encouraged to do that for themselves?

ROSEMARY LAIN-PRIESTLEY

Mary, the mother of Jesus

When [Jesus'] parents saw him they were astonished; and his mother said to him, 'Child, why have you treated us like this? Look, your father and I have been searching for you in great anxiety.' He said to them, 'Why were you searching for me? Did you not know that I must be in my Father's house?' But they did not understand what he said to them.

One of the most difficult things about parenting is discerning the point at which our children can be responsible for themselves. That concern for them is a particularly acute challenge during their adolescence, but it begins at the moment they are born and, I am told, does not end when they become adults!

Mary faced her own acute version of that challenge throughout Jesus' life. Barely knowing what she was doing, she summoned the courage to say 'Yes' to God's request, she shared the puzzlement and frustration of all parents as her son grew separate from her in his very singular way. She was in the background, wanting him to come home, and she stayed until the end, summoning indescribable courage to watch his unspeakable death.

What do we learn from her? We learn that all of us have the capacity to embrace the challenge of the miraculous, although our understanding of what it might mean will, at the start, be limited. We learn that to love anyone unreservedly must involve pain and that saying 'Yes' to God involves risk. We learn that God's purposes in the world were fulfilled as a result of the courage, persistence and love of a woman about whom we barely know anything, most of whose words are lost to history.

The risk of nurturing anything through the processes of birth and growth has much in common with the risk of saying 'Yes' to God. Both will lead us to new places in ourselves. Within the hazards and challenge lie miracle and wonder and so, with Mary, we say 'Yes'.

Prayer

Thank you, God, that you work in the world not by using force or might, but in relationship with all those who have the courage to hear your call. Nurture that courage in me, so I may risk saying 'Yes'. Amen

ROSEMARY LAIN-PRIESTLEY

The woman who anointed Jesus

[Jesus] said to Simon, 'Do you see this woman? I entered your house; you gave me no water for my feet, but she has bathed my feet with her tears and dried them with her hair. You gave me no kiss, but from the time I came in she has not stopped kissing my feet. You did not anoint my head with oil, but she has anointed my feet with ointment.'

Poor Simon the Pharisee! He may have expected some flak from his colleagues for inviting Jesus to dinner, but he would not have anticipated that his guest would rate his hospitality so low. 'No water, no kiss, no oil', Jesus observed. It was unfortunate for Simon that the woman who crashed his party was so extravagant in her attentiveness, so passionate in her fragility, that she prompted the parable following these verses, in which Simon became the ungrateful debtor and she the one pregnant with faith and love.

Any of us could be a Pharisee like Simon—reticent, bound by social convention, wary of otherness and difference. We could, instead, choose to be the woman—intuitive and perceptive in her vulnerability, seeing to the heart of things and responding with passion. Given particular circumstances, we take our place in either corner in our encounters with God and relationships with one another. This woman who anointed Jesus offers us a breathtaking picture of how we might relate more intimately to God—holding back nothing, pouring out all that we are and all we have, letting ourselves go in order to let God in.

Are we going to be the ones to whom God says, 'You were so uptight, so distracted, so full of fear that you gave me no water, no kiss, no anointing; and neither did you do that for each other' or, in the knowledge of all that we have been forgiven, will we say 'Yes' to God's touch and invitation?

Prayer

Lord, sometimes I am more comfortable with you at a distance
and more comfortable with myself when I am contained and in control.
Help me to trust myself to your intimate love and trust others with the
person I am in you. Amen

ROSEMARY LAIN-PRIESTLEY

Mary of Magdala

Supposing him to be the gardener, [Mary] said to him, 'Sir, if you have carried him away, tell me where you have laid him, and I will take him away.' Jesus said to her, 'Mary!' She turned and said to him in Hebrew, 'Rabbouni!' (which means Teacher). Jesus said to her, 'Do not hold on to me, because I have not yet ascended to the Father. But go to my brothers.'

When Jesus first met Mary of Magdala, she was in a very bad way. The ancient writers describe her as being possessed by seven demons (Luke 8:2), but today we might describe her as suffering from a complex personality disorder. There is no mention of her family and she seems very much alone.

Jesus heals Mary and she suddenly has a new way of being. Having had nothing but her torturing demons for company, she now experiences the unconditional love of God and life among an itinerant group of friends. She has more than survived what was threatening to destroy her.

Then, all of this is seemingly taken away. We meet her here the day after the crucifixion, begging at least to have the body, to take him back to herself, if it is all that is left. Jesus, however, offers her much more—his risen self, released into the world, dwelling in the very fissures of creation and in Mary herself and the other believers.

His body, neither the dead nor the risen one, is not for her. She cannot hold on to him that way. She has to let go and stand upright in the strength of his risen reality. What Jesus knows is that Mary is so filled with the truth of divine love and healing, she is now well enough to take this gift to the world. He sends her out as the first witness of his resurrection.

Reflection

God is wholly gift and that gift cannot be controlled or pinned down or it will lose its power to change things and its capacity to surprise. Remind yourself that, in your very depths, which God has prepared, you do know his presence and you carry it wherever you go.

ROSEMARY LAIN-PRIESTLEY

Women of the early church

I commend to you our sister Phoebe, a deacon of the church at Cenchreae, so that you may welcome her in the Lord as is fitting for the saints, and help her in whatever she may require from you, for she has been a benefactor of many and of myself as well. Greet Prisca and Aquila... Greet Andronicus and Junia, my relatives who were in prison with me; they are prominent among the apostles.

Gender politics in the church can give the impression that women have only recently occupied public roles in Christian faith communities. The Acts of the Apostles and Paul's letters strongly suggest otherwise.

Phoebe was a deacon and benefactor in a church near Corinth. She acted as Paul's emissary in taking his letter to the believers in Rome and then stayed with them, probably to discuss its contents. Prisca and her husband Aquila were tentmakers, like Paul, and, in Acts 18:26, are equally credited with instructing the evangelist Apollos and correcting his interpretation of the gospel. Then we have Junia, who had been imprisoned with Paul. Perhaps because of Paul's reference to her prominence among the apostles, her name was masculinised to Junias by some early translators. In 1 Corinthians 1:10–11, there is a householder named Chloe, whom many historians believe to have led a house church.

In Acts 16:13–15, we meet Paul's friend Lydia, a trader in expensive purple cloth who lived in Philippi. She put her resources at Paul's disposal, probably contributing to the spread of his mission around the Mediterranean by her contacts and knowledge of shipping companies.

These women had networks and connections as a result of work and social relationships and considerable physical and intellectual gifts to offer. They were resource-rich and resourceful and influenced the way in which the gospel was propagated, both in their domestic contexts and across the ancient world. They are role models for all of us, women and men, as we live out that gospel today.

Reflection

Who are today's role models who offer their resources in the service of the kingdom, either quietly and locally or more visibly on a global stage? How might we be encouraged by their stories to use our own God-given gifts?

ROSEMARY LAIN-PRIESTLEY

Light and darkness: John 8—9

Of the four Gospel writers, John is the most intuitive. He writes reflectively, choosing his words carefully for their depth of meaning, and enjoys using metaphors and symbolism rather than simply recounting facts and details. This makes his Gospel ideal for meditation.

John is selective in the stories he records, preferring those with a 'double' meaning—that is, they are records of actual events, but also illustrate deeper truth. Thus, the miracles in John are called 'signs'. They are not simply demonstrations of God's power but also parables filled with spiritual meaning, pointing us in the direction of the truth. So, the feeding of the five thousand leads naturally into the declaration by Jesus that he is the bread of life (John 6:35).

The contrast between light and darkness is one of the most prominent themes used by John—a symbolism that goes right back to the creation of the world. Light represents the knowledge of God, whereas darkness represents the ignorance that comes from not knowing him. In the two chapters we are going to consider in the notes that follow—8 and 9—this contrast is explored at length.

Chapter 8 begins with the deeply moving story of the woman caught in adultery and the attempt made by the Pharisees to trick Jesus into contradicting the Law. He counteracts their strategy by exposing the sin in their hearts (darkness) and offering to the woman forgiveness and a chance to start again (light). It is in this context that he makes the declaration, 'I am the light of the world' (8:12). Exactly what he is claiming by this statement then becomes the subject of a lengthy and complicated debate.

Chapter 9 begins with the healing of a man born blind. This story becomes the basis of further understanding of Jesus as the light of the world (9:5) and the nature of spiritual blindness. In the various responses of people to the miracle, we are given an insight into their spiritual condition, whether they are in the light or still in darkness.

As we read, we are challenged to think about our own spiritual sight and consider our need for the illumination that Jesus brings. Perhaps we also need a healing touch for the eyes of our heart (Ephesians 1:18).

Tony Horsfall

Light and darkness

The teachers of the law and the Pharisees brought in a woman caught in adultery. They made her stand before the group and said to Jesus, 'Teacher, this woman was caught in the act of adultery. In the Law Moses commanded us to stone such women. Now what do you say?' They were using this question as a trap, in order to have a basis for accusing him. But Jesus bent down and started to write on the ground with his finger.

John's Gospel begins with a statement about the birth of Jesus: 'The true light that gives light to every man was coming into the world' (1:9). It also says that not everyone welcomed the coming of the light: 'The light shines in the darkness, but the darkness has not understood it' (1:5).

This theme, of the clash between light and darkness, is played out throughout John's Gospel, but especially so in this chapter and in this incident. We may readily associate spiritual darkness with Satan, but not necessarily with religious people, yet here, in the behaviour and motivation of the Pharisees, we see darkness at work.

First, it can be seen in the harsh way they treat this poor woman. She is publicly humiliated in the name of God. In all likelihood, her offence came to light through an act of entrapment, as the man is not brought to account. These self-righteous teachers of the Law are ready to stone her without any understanding of her situation or compassion on her plight.

Second, it is seen in their scheming to trap Jesus into speaking contrary to the Law so that they can discredit him. The whole thing is a set-up, a crafty, underhanded ploy to defame him and counteract his influence. They are determined not to believe for themselves (7:48–49) and to discourage others also.

Jesus, however, is wise to their tricks. We do not know what he wrote in the sand, but his unspoken words seem to have begun a process of individual enlightenment in their hardened hearts. How sad it is when those who should bring light to others actually, in their ignorance and prejudice, pass on darkness.

Prayer
Lord, where there is darkness may we bring your light.

TONY HORSFALL

JOHN 8:7–11 (NIV)

The light shines

When they kept on questioning him, he straightened up and said to them, 'Let any one of you who is without sin be the first to throw a stone at her.' Again he stooped down and wrote on the ground. At this, those who heard began to go away one at a time, the older ones first, until only Jesus was left, with the woman still standing there. Jesus straightened up and asked her, 'Woman, where are they? Has no one condemned you?' 'No one, sir,' she said. 'Then neither do I condemn you,' Jesus declared. 'Go now and leave your life of sin.'

The words of Jesus penetrate both the accusers and the condemned deeply. To the first they bring challenge and rebuke, to the second healing and hope. Into the darkness of self-righteousness Jesus says, 'If any one of you is without sin, let him be the first to throw a stone at her' (v. 7).

Did Jesus' writing in the sand expose some personal indiscretions of this group of powerful men or are they simply convicted by the Holy Spirit? Either way, they are made to face up to their own shortcomings and, one by one, they slink away in shame. Perhaps the older ones move first because they have more history of failure than the young who have still to be tested.

Then, into the darkness of guilt, shame and painful humiliation, Jesus speaks a word of pure, shining grace: 'Has no one condemned you?… neither do I' (vv. 10–11). His words bring forgiveness and cleansing, the assurance of being accepted and loved despite failure and weakness. They bring with them the power to change and the possibility of a new beginning: 'Go now and leave your life of sin ' (v. 11).

People often fear coming into the light, but Jesus intends only to liberate us. The dawning of self-awareness can be painful, but change is not possible until we have seen and acknowledged our own darkness. To stand exposed and convicted would be frightening unless we discovered in that moment the unconditional love of God. Then it is healing and releasing, for there is no more need to hide.

Prayer

Lord, may I have courage to welcome the spotlight of your love.

TONY HORSFALL

Jesus the light of the world

> When Jesus spoke again to the people, he said, 'I am the light of the world. Whoever follows me will never walk in darkness, but will have the light of life.' The Pharisees challenged him, 'Here you are, appearing as your own witness; your testimony is not valid.' Jesus answered, 'Even if I testify on my own behalf, my testimony is valid, for I know where I came from and where I am going. But you have no idea where I come from or where I am going.'

This is the second of seven 'I am' sayings of Jesus, declarations that he made about his identity that are also indicators of his divinity (the others are 6:35; 10:9, 11; 11:25; 14:6; 15:1). The Pharisees refuse to accept such self-generated testimony, not because his claim is false, but because they lack the spiritual discernment to recognise its validity.

In what sense is Jesus 'the light of the world'? By coming in the flesh, he has made God fully known (John 1:18), thus dispelling the darkness of ignorance about what God is like. By his life, he makes God visible and, by his words, he makes God understandable. Thus, he fulfils the prophecy of Isaiah: 'The people walking in darkness have seen a great light' (9:2). This he does for the whole world and for all peoples, not just for Israel and the Jews.

His appearance involves a summons to follow him and become his disciples. This is an invitation to forsake the darkness of sin and ignorance about God and step into the light of the knowledge of God that he imparts. This call to faith is the reason for John writing his Gospel (20:30–31), while the challenge to believe is a constant theme.

For those willing to follow Jesus, there is the promise of 'the light of life'. No longer will such people stumble around in the darkness, not knowing how to live and with no guiding principle. Rather, they will see clearly what is important, understand right from wrong and have the wisdom to make good decisions. By his example and teaching, Jesus will guide them through the maze of life.

Reflection

'The Lord is my light and my salvation' (Psalm 27:1).

TONY HORSFALL

Who are you?

Once more Jesus said to them, 'I am going away, and you will look for me, and you will die in your sin. Where I go, you cannot come.' This made the Jews ask, 'Will he kill himself? Is that why he says, "Where I go, you cannot come"?' But he continued, 'You are from below; I am from above. You are of this world; I am not of this world…' 'Who are you?' they asked. 'Just what I have been telling you from the beginning,' Jesus replied.

Although Jesus came to his own people, they did not recognise who he was and so did not welcome him. In his home town of Nazareth, they rejected him, for all they could see was a carpenter's son (Mark 6:1–5). Even his own brothers did not believe in him (John 7:5). For most people, Jesus remained an enigma and, like many of the Jews, their question was simply, 'Who are you?'

In this context it is not surprising that, when Jesus speaks of his heavenly origin ('I am from above') and his forthcoming death ('I am going away'), his listeners are completely baffled. He is speaking the language of faith, but they are limited to human understanding; he is communicating spiritual truth, but they can only grasp what their natural minds can fathom.

This does not mean that Jesus was playing games with them or trying to conceal his identity, but, for those who could only see things from a human standpoint, his true identity remained a mystery. Only those with 'ears to hear' could grasp the meaning of his parables and only those willing to humble themselves and become like little children were able to penetrate the mysteries of the kingdom.

Without the help of the Spirit of God, none of us can discern spiritual truth and we remain in darkness (Matthew 11:25–26; 1 Corinthians 2:14). It is a reminder to ask humbly that our eyes may be opened so that we can appreciate who Jesus is and comprehend the things he has to say. Then we will no longer be in darkness, but can live in the light of God.

Prayer
Lighten our darkness we beseech thee, O Lord.

From the Third Collect, The Order for Evening Prayer, Book of Common Prayer

TONY HORSFALL

When I am lifted up

[Jesus said] 'I have much to say in judgement of you. But he who sent me is trustworthy, and what I have heard from him I tell the world.' They did not understand that he was telling them about his Father. So Jesus said, 'When you have lifted up the Son of Man, then you will know that I am he and that I do nothing on my own but speak just what the Father has taught me. The one who sent me is with me; he has not left me alone, for I always do what pleases him.' Even as he spoke, many believed in him.

The relationship between Jesus and the Father is a prominent feature of John's Gospel. More than any other writer, John reveals the depth of intimacy that existed between the Son and the Father. Here we see two aspects of that deep communion.

Jesus came not to proclaim his own truth but to speak the words of the Father. He was careful not to act independently of the Father ('I do nothing on my own') and to say only what the Father gave him to say ('what the Father has taught me') (v. 28). He lived to please the Father.

In all his ministry, he was conscious of the supporting presence of the Father. Even when misunderstood by his hearers, let down by his followers or attacked by his opponents, he was able to remain strong because he was never alone. Having been sent by the Father, he was upheld by the Father.

Here, Jesus speaks calmly of his forthcoming death in terms that prefigure the crucifixion and see it as a result of Jewish opposition ('when *you* have lifted up the Son of Man', v. 28, emphasis added). He can face such a future ordeal calmly because of the depth of the communion he enjoys with the Father.

Something about his words and his assurance speak deeply to those of his listeners who remain open-minded and willing to believe. Indeed, many then put their faith in him. While religious leaders are blind, the simple-hearted can see; what is hidden from the wise is revealed to babes.

Prayer

Lord, help me to grow in communion with the Father.

TONY HORSFALL

True freedom

To the Jews who had believed him, Jesus said, 'If you hold to my teaching, you are really my disciples. Then you will know the truth, and the truth will set you free.' They answered him, 'We are Abraham's descendants and have never been slaves of anyone. How can you say that we shall be set free?' Jesus replied, 'Very truly I tell you, everyone who sins is a slave to sin. Now a slave has no permanent place in the family, but a son belongs to it for ever. So if the Son sets you free, you will be free indeed.'

Jesus begins immediately to teach these new disciples and we can assume that his words here are of paramount importance to any new believer who would build on a good foundation. To grow as a disciple of Jesus we must be set free from anything that would prevent us from loving God with all our hearts.

Notice that it is the truth that sets us free. We must know the truth about ourselves, as painful as that may be. The light of God must shine into our hearts and expose our wrongdoing. We cannot afford to deceive ourselves or pretend that we are better than we are. We may be tempted, like these new followers, to hide behind our spiritual ancestry (or, as we would put it today, our church affiliation, Christian upbringing and so on), but we are all slaves to sin in one way or another.

Notice, too, that it is Jesus, the Son of Man, who sets us free. Not only is he the one who shines the light of gospel truth into our darkened hearts but he is also the one who administers the forgiving and cleansing grace of God to heal our sin-sick souls. Just as he spoke forgiveness to the woman caught in the act of adultery, so he speaks forgiveness to each of us in whom his light shines. When the Son sets us free, we will be free indeed—completely, totally, absolutely forgiven.

Whatever stage you have reached on your Christian journey, never fear the truth of God. It will always set you free.

Prayer
Lord, help me to walk in the light.

TONY HORSFALL

Before Abraham was born, I am

Jesus replied, 'If I glorify myself, my glory means nothing. My Father, whom you claim as your God, is the one who glorifies me... Your father Abraham rejoiced at the thought of seeing my day; he saw it and was glad.' 'You are not yet fifty years old,' they said to him, 'and you have seen Abraham!' 'Very truly I tell you,' Jesus answered, 'before Abraham was born, I am!' At this, they picked up stones to stone him, but Jesus hid himself, slipping away from the temple grounds.

The rather heated discussion about the identity of Jesus continues, but now, like some highly charged political campaign, things begin to get personal. Jesus is accused of being illegitimate, a Samaritan and then demon-possessed (vv. 41, 48). Although they still find it hard to understand all he says, they realise he is claiming to be sent from God and that God is his Father. 'Who do you think you are?' they ask indignantly (v. 53).

Much of the discussion has centred on the importance of Abraham and the fact that he is the father of the Jews. Abraham was a man of faith, with spiritual insight and, as such, was able to look ahead to what God would do in the future. He had been promised that not only would he have a son but also many descendants (Genesis 15:4–5) and all nations would be blessed because of him (12:2–3). That day has now arrived and, in the coming of Jesus ('my day', v. 56), the promises are fulfilled and Abraham will be rejoicing (Galatians 3:8–9, 14).

There is more truth, however, and it is even harder to grasp. Since Jesus is himself divine, he existed before Abraham. The claim 'before Abraham was born, I am' (John 8:58) is unmistakably a claim to pre-existence and equality with God. The Jews are infuriated and pick up stones to kill the blasphemer. So, this chapter began with Jesus preventing a stoning and ends, ironically, with him slipping away to avoid his own. This is not the time for his death or the way in which he will die.

Reflection

'If God were your Father, you would love me, for I came from God and now am here' (8:42).

TONY HORSFALL

A man born blind

As [Jesus] went along, he saw a man blind from birth. His disciples asked him, 'Rabbi, who sinned, this man or his parents, that he was born blind?' 'Neither this man nor his parents sinned,' said Jesus, 'but this happened so that the works of God might be displayed in him. As long as it is day, we must do the works of him who sent me. Night is coming, when no one can work. While I am in the world, I am the light of the world.'

It seems as if meeting the blind man was a chance encounter and it may well have been, but John sees deep significance in the ensuing story. It will result in more than a physical healing, remarkable and faith-building though that is in itself. It will become a drama about spiritual insight and discernment and the obstacles to seeing and recognising the work of God.

The disciples, by asking this question, show how our theological framework or worldview can prevent us from apprehending the truth. Their understanding is that conditions such as blindness are caused by sin, so this man must be blind because either he or his parents had sinned. Their logic may or may not be at fault, but their starting premise is, and so Jesus corrects their basic assumption: no one is to blame for the man's blindness and his condition is not the result of sin. In fact, God is going to use the man's life circumstances to reveal his glory. His healing will be the means by which God's truth will be seen and will be a way by which the claim that Jesus is the light of the world is confirmed.

To ask, 'Who sinned?' is therefore to ask the wrong question. A better one would be, 'What is God doing in this situation?' Rather than looking for someone to blame for his unfortunate condition, those who have eyes to see will be able to recognise the hand of God at work in the man's life and see his glory being displayed.

We must beware holding our beliefs so tightly that we leave no room for God to surprise us.

Prayer
May the works of God be displayed in my life.

TONY HORSFALL

Coming home seeing

Having said this, he spat on the ground, made some mud with the saliva, and put it on the man's eyes. 'Go,' he told him, 'wash in the Pool of Siloam' (this word means 'Sent'). So the man went and washed, and came home seeing. His neighbours and those who had formerly seen him begging asked, 'Isn't this the same man who used to sit and beg?' Some claimed that he was. Others said, 'No, he only looks like him.' But he himself insisted, 'I am the man.'

We cannot be certain why Jesus put mud on the man's eyes or asked him to wash in the Pool of Siloam when he could have healed him simply by touching him. Perhaps the first act was to encourage his faith and the second to help him express his faith. Certainly the man takes Jesus at his word and, as he responds in obedience, a miracle occurs—he comes home seeing. What an amazing moment in the life of one born blind.

His neighbours, surprisingly, are not sure if he is the same person who has lived among them for so long. They had seen him every day as he sat there begging, yet most of them had never 'seen' him at all. He was a person of no consequence, a nobody, and they had taken little notice of him. He was simply part of the background to their everyday lives, so now many of them fail to register the miraculous because they cannot confidently identify the man. Perhaps they think it might be a scam or a confidence trick. Despite the man's protestations, some are hesitant to acknowledge that the man they knew to be blind has been healed.

Familiarity prevented the people of Nazareth from recognising that Jesus was more than the carpenter's son (Matthew 13:53–57). Daily familiarity with the blind beggar and his circumstances prevented some people from seeing the glory of God at work in their neighbour's life. They never expected anything special to happen to him, let alone for him to be healed.

Let each of us take care, lest we, too, limit what we believe God can do, by setting our expectations too low.

Prayer

Lord, let nothing deaden my hope of seeing your glory.

TONY HORSFALL

From God or not?

> They brought to the Pharisees the man who had been blind. Now the day on which Jesus had made the mud and opened the man's eyes was a Sabbath. Therefore the Pharisees also asked him how he had received his sight. 'He put mud on my eyes,' the man replied, 'and I washed, and now I see.' Some of the Pharisees said, 'This man is not from God, for he does not keep the Sabbath.' But others asked, 'How can a sinner do such signs?' So they were divided.

Who brought the man to the Pharisees? Perhaps his neighbours, keen to have the miracle verified by the religious authorities. These men, however, have their own blindspots—assumptions that prevent them from recognising a genuine act of God.

For the Pharisees, the stumbling block is that this miracle happened on the sabbath, a day when no work was to be done. Did Jesus deliberately choose the sabbath day to heal the man to provoke them? Their reasoning was simple. If God commanded there to be no work on the sabbath and someone heals on the sabbath, then that man is a sinner and cannot be from God. There is no rejoicing in the good that has been done, only a frosty denunciation of breaking the sabbath.

Their approach to the sabbath was so strict and their definition of what constituted work so tight that they had left no room for God to work in his own world. A child could be circumcised, but a blind man could not be healed (John 7:21–24). Their attachment to the sabbath traditions excluded even acts of compassion. This also provided a convenient excuse for dismissing the claims of Jesus and a plausible way of defending and strengthening their own position.

Not all are immune to the truth or as resistant to the light, however. Those who are more open-minded and humble hesitate to dismiss Jesus as a sinner. For them, future enlightenment remains a possibility.

The truth is not always convenient. Sometimes it disturbs the status quo and challenges our belief systems and practices. Then our response shows whether we love the light or not (John 3:19–21).

Prayer
Grant me courage to pursue the truth regardless of the cost.

TONY HORSFALL

Because they were afraid

[The Jewish leaders] still did not believe that he had been blind and had received his sight until they sent for the man's parents. 'Is this your son?' they asked. 'Is this the one you say was born blind? How is it that now he can see?' 'We know he is our son,' the parents answered, 'and we know he was born blind. But how he can see now, or who opened his eyes, we don't know. Ask him. He is of age; he will speak for himself.' His parents said this because they were afraid of the Jewish leaders, who had already decided that anyone who acknowledged that Jesus was the Messiah would be put out of the synagogue.

The spotlight now falls on the man's parents and they are uncomfortable in the glare of this public attention. What should have been a day of family celebration turns into a traumatic confrontation with the religious authorities, of whom they are deeply afraid. They know the truth, but fear causes them to betray their son and their own consciences.

Religious leaders have great power and sometimes exercise it wrongly. Already the Pharisees had decided that anyone who acknowledged the true identity of Jesus would be put out of the synagogue. The threat of such public humiliation and social ostracism is too great for this humble couple to contemplate and they crumble under the pressure. Rather than standing up for their son and recognising what God had done for him, they back away and pass the responsibility over to him.

Truth can only flourish in a context in which people are free to express themselves without fear of there being consequences if they fail to toe the party line. Christian congregations should especially be places where we allow people such freedom, for only then will we be able to recognise and discern the will of God together. When truth is suppressed, the work of God will be restricted.

All of us must have the courage and humility to stay open to the truth, wherever it is found. We must never intimidate others into silence because we ourselves are afraid of the truth.

Prayer

Grant us grace, Lord, to love the truth and act in love.

TONY HORSFALL

One thing I know

A second time they summoned the man who had been blind. 'Give glory to God by telling the truth,' they said. 'We know this man is a sinner.' He replied, 'Whether he is a sinner or not, I don't know. One thing I do know. I was blind but now I see!' Then they asked him, 'What did he do to you? How did he open your eyes?' He answered, 'I have told you already and you did not listen. Why do you want to hear it again? Do you want to become his disciples, too?'

Having browbeaten the parents, the Pharisees now turn their attention to the man himself, hoping to silence him as well. How ironic it is to hear them urge him to give glory to God when that is the very thing they will not do themselves.

This man is from a very humble background and, having been blind since birth, will have had little education or social status to bolster his self-confidence, especially when called to account before such an intimidating body of people. Yet, he is clear in his testimony and unafraid in his response: 'One thing I do know. I was blind but now I see' (v. 25).

There is nothing as convincing as the power of personal testimony. This poor man knew well that he had been born blind and lived all his life up to this point in total darkness, with no visual images of the world around him. He also knew that now he could see and see as clearly as anyone else—the sun, the sky, the trees, the people around him, the buildings, even himself. There must have been so much for him to take in, so much for him to enjoy and marvel at, so much to rejoice over and yet he finds himself accused, as if he had done wrong.

He is no match intellectually for the Pharisees, but the evidence of his healing is there for all to see and cannot be denied. For him, the implication is clear: he must become a disciple of Jesus. For these disciples of Moses, however, such a conclusion is unthinkable. Somehow they must suppress this truth.

Reflection

What is your testimony?

TONY HORSFALL

He listens to the godly

[They said] 'We know that God spoke to Moses, but as for this fellow, we don't even know where he comes from.' The man answered, 'Now that is remarkable! You don't know where he comes from, yet he opened my eyes. We know that God does not listen to sinners. He listens to the godly person who does his will. Nobody has ever heard of opening the eyes of a man born blind. If this man were not from God, he could do nothing.'... And they threw him out.

We are again amazed at the boldness given to the man who has been healed in the face of such fierce intimidation. We are also amazed to see another example of how harsh and brutal the Pharisees could be in their treatment of people. They appear to be heading further and further into the darkness because of their stubborn refusal to recognise the healing as an act of God.

The man may not have been educated in the Torah, nor had the religious training that his interrogators had had, but his theology, as simple as it is, is accurate: 'if this man were not from God, he could do nothing' (v. 33). What he can see in his simplicity, they in their sophistication cannot. The truth is hidden from their eyes because of their allegiance as disciples of Moses to their party line. Spiritual truth is indeed kept from the wise and learned and revealed to little children (Matthew 11:25).

The man pays a high price for his commitment to the truth and is thrown out of their meeting. It is never easy to stand alone, be misunderstood or swim against the tide; far easier to stay with the group, think the same as everyone else and avoid rocking the boat. The easy way, however, is not necessarily the right way, and 'groupthink' or peer pressure can blind us to the truth of God.

How do we respond when God does something we have not experienced before? Can we step outside of our frame of reference and recognise the work of God or are we locked into a particular way of thinking?

Prayer
Lord, keep me humble and teachable.

TONY HORSFALL

Journey into the light

Jesus heard that they had thrown him out, and when he found him, he said, 'Do you believe in the Son of Man?' 'Who is he, sir?' the man asked. 'Tell me so that I may believe in him.' Jesus said, 'You have now seen him; in fact, he is the one speaking with you.' Then the man said, 'Lord, I believe,' and he worshipped him.

In the tender way Jesus comes and looks for the man after his cruel expulsion we see the loving heart of the good shepherd.

God is at work in the man in two ways: restoring his physical sight, and opening the 'eyes of his heart' to grasp spiritual truth. It must have taken him some time to start seeing again properly, and it took time for him to grasp the true identity of his healer.

As we read through the story, we can trace his growing understanding and his pathway to faith. At first, he can only speak of 'the man they call Jesus' (v. 11). This suggests that he had heard about Jesus before his healing, but knew very little about him.

Then, after being questioned about his healer and forced to think more about what had happened to him, he tells the Pharisees, 'He is a prophet' (v. 17). Anyone responsible for such a miracle has to be special and, at this point, the category of 'prophet' seems appropriate.

His understanding is deepening all the time and further probing from the Pharisees draws from him the growing conviction that his healer must be a man sent from God, otherwise he could heal no one (v. 33).

Now, when Jesus comes and finds him and speaks to him, he recognises that Jesus is much more than a prophet: he is the Son of Man. It is the last step of the journey to faith. Without hesitation, he declares, 'I believe' and there and then worships him.

John uses this story to remind us that we are all on a journey and faith comes to us in stages. If we are committed to following the light that Jesus gives, it will bring us eventually to God.

Prayer
Lord, help us to grow in faith and assurance.

TONY HORSFALL

Are we blind, too?

Jesus said, 'For judgement I have come into this world, so that the blind will see and those who see will become blind.' Some Pharisees who were with him heard him say this and asked, 'What? Are we blind too?' Jesus said, 'If you were blind, you would not be guilty of sin; but now that you claim you can see, your guilt remains.'

The thrust of the two chapters we have read (John 8 and 9) has been about spiritual discernment, having eyes to see what God is doing and the faith to respond accordingly. The healing of the man born blind gives us confidence to believe that Jesus is powerful enough to help us even in the most difficult circumstances, but his story also illustrates for us the spiritual journey—the movement from being blind to what God is doing to seeing him at work all around us. The healing also acts as a catalyst to reveal where different people are on this journey.

In order to increase our capacity to recognise the work of God and discern his will, we need to remain teachable and humble, open to any fresh wind of the Spirit. This is what the Pharisees were unable to do. Locked into a system of religious belief and practice, they were closed in their thinking and, therefore, blind in their seeing. They had a vested interest in maintaining the status quo and used their power and influence to suppress the truth. When God came to them in Jesus, they resisted his teaching and turned away from the light. They could not bring themselves to admit that they might be wrong or have something more to learn.

True discernment begins when we acknowledge that we may not be seeing well and need divine intervention. It continues as we recognise that God may be bigger than our present way of thinking and open ourselves to change.

All of us need the light of life that Jesus brings. There is more for us to learn, more darkness for him to dispel. He alone is the light of the world.

Prayer

Lord, may I always be open, humble and honest in my response to you.

TONY HORSFALL

The Servant Songs of Isaiah

What do we do when we find ourselves in exile from something, some-one or even everything that we know and love? This is the tough question that runs through the Servant Songs of Isaiah and explains why, even now, a song book some 2500 years old has the potential to get us singing ourselves and the world around us into a new way of being.

The Servant Songs are a series of iconic passages within the pro-phetic writings of the Jewish scriptures that we know as Isaiah. They actually fall, for the most part, within the writings known as Deutero-Isaiah, or, Second Isaiah—reflecting a common understanding that chapters 40—55 were written by a different author from the one(s) who wrote chapters 1—39 (Proto-Isaiah) and the one(s) who wrote 56—66 (Trito-Isaiah). (In the following notes we will also spend time with a passage from chapter 61, which some understand to be an additional Servant Song.)

Second Isaiah is dated to the catastrophic exile of the Jewish people in Babylon after 587BC and perhaps more specifically to the period around 540BC when under the threat of further calamity in the shape of an impending Assyrian invasion of Babylon.

A key question for scholars has been to identify who is the servant who sings the songs. We will give that question some attention—but whoever the servant was for the writer, there exists the possibility that we are now invited to join our own voices to the Servant Songs.

If we imagine the whole of Second Isaiah as an opera of exile and homecoming, the Servant Songs are perhaps the arias of the one through whom God's new thing will be sung into being. There is a sense of the impossibility of what is about to unfold. Change seems impossible, the Empire rules—and yet…

So how might we best engage with the Servant Songs? This needs to be done both communally and personally and is perhaps best approached in question form. How might these texts shape us as a people, community or church—and how might you and I sing the Servant Song wherever we are today, whatever we face?

Ian Adams

The song will be sung again

> Here is my servant, whom I uphold, my chosen, in whom my soul delights; I have put my spirit upon him; he will bring forth justice to the nations.

In tough times we can easily lose our voice. The song falls back into the pit of our stomach, it sticks in the throat or is lost as it escapes from our lips. In the opening passage of the first of the Servant Songs, we are given a glimpse into why the servant in Isaiah may be able to sing even in exile. The servant is being upheld, chosen by God and delighted in by God and God's spirit is upon him, so that he may 'bring forth justice to the nations' (v. 1). God is inspiring the song of salvation and it will be sung again!

If the song is to be sung, however, who is to sing it? Who is the servant? Is he a specific individual, a special anointed one? Could it be the prophet Isaiah himself or the prophet's disciple community? Perhaps it is the whole people of Israel or a righteous remnant within Israel? The consensus seems to be that links to all of the above may be found in the person of the servant.

Of course, for Christians, the servant has long been identified with Jesus the Messiah. Here we pick up early resonances with a key moment in the life of Jesus—his baptism by John in the Jordan. Revealed beneath the upholding, the choosing and the delighting in is something even more far-reaching—the love of God for this servant. 'This is my Son', says the voice from heaven, 'the Beloved, with whom I am well pleased' (Matthew 3:17). From this place of belovedness, Jesus' calling takes on new clarity, strength and possibility.

The scriptures always have the capacity to reach beyond their original time and audience, so the possibility of our being loved, upheld, chosen and delighted in begins to surface. We, too, may be servants who will sing the song.

Reflection

Reflect on your sense of belovedness—or otherwise—at this time. Do not be afraid to voice what you feel. Let this become a prayer.

IAN ADAMS

A quiet revolution

He will not cry or lift up his voice, or make it heard in the street; a bruised reed he will not break, and a dimly burning wick he will not quench; he will faithfully bring forth justice. He will not grow faint or be crushed until he has established justice in the earth; and the coastlands wait for his teaching.

The first Servant Song contains a surprise. Both the song and the 'justice for the nations' (v. 1) that the song will usher in will be of a different quality from what might be expected in a long struggle for justice. This will be a quiet movement, perhaps seemingly insignificant, containing a gentle respect for others. Already, bruised reeds will not be broken, dimly burning wicks will not be extinguished. This will be a gentle revolution that will sweep up both those who see the need for it and those who as yet do not.

How unexpected this must have sounded to the first people who heard these words in exile. Surely only a massive armed force could overthrow the Babylonian empire at this time. What could a relatively small and dispirited group of exiles, collaborators and slaves do in the face of the might of this empire?

This raises for us a dilemma in any struggle for justice. How can we resist what is wrong without becoming like whatever we are resisting? This will take humility, self-awareness and love, but this approach must not be mistaken for being soft. This bringing of justice will also be persistent. It will become clear that people—the coastlands—are hungry for a return to this type of persistent salvation.

Perhaps this is what Jesus had in heart and mind when he taught—in the context of another great and mighty empire—'Blessed are the meek, for they will inherit the earth' (Matthew 5:5). Only the meek have the character to bring true justice.

Reflection

What are the injustices that you are confronting at this time? How might a quiet but persistent song of resistance sound coming from your mouth? How might it shape your work for justice at this time?

Ian Adams

Prepared for the song of justice

Listen to me, O coastlands, pay attention, you peoples from far away! The Lord called me before I was born, while I was in my mother's womb he named me. He made my mouth like a sharp sword, in the shadow of his hand he hid me; he made me a polished arrow, in his quiver he hid me away. And he said to me, 'You are my servant, Israel, in whom I will be glorified.'

In the first of the Servant Songs the voice we hear is that of God. At the beginning of this, the second of the Servant Songs, a new singer takes up the song. Here, for the first time, we hear the servant, and the words reveal this singer's sense that the song has deep roots in his past. There is a wider, longer, deeper purpose here. The singer has been called long before he was born. He was named for the task in his mother's womb and his mouth and voice have been 'sharpened' and readied for this task.

To sing the song is the servant's calling. He has been prepared, away from public view, and now the moment has come. His rootedness in God's calling will enable him to sing the song of justice in exile, however daunting the task may seem. We can see this kind of process in the lives of those we know have fought for justice. Nelson Mandela is an obvious example—incarcerated for many years, exiled from society, all the time nurturing a humble sense of his calling and destiny and finally able to sing the song of justice when the moment came. Mandela's actions were a gift to the world, but his story is perhaps also a personal gift to each one of us, alerting us to the possibility that we, too, have been called, readied and equipped to sing the justice song right where we are.

Reflection

What do you sense might be your calling at this time? Putting your own name to that calling, as the servant does, is a powerful thing. In God's care, may you have the courage to do so today.

Ian Adams

Lost calling?

> But I said, 'I have laboured in vain, I have spent my strength for nothing and vanity; yet surely my cause is with the Lord, and my reward with my God.'

The unfinished draft of a letter was found on the body of the artist Vincent van Gogh when he died, largely ignored as an artist, in July 1890. The letter included this line: 'As for my own work. I risk my life for it and my sanity is half shot away because of it...'.

If you have ever experienced the apparent failure of a calling that once seemed to have been clear, blessed and full of promise, you will know how deep and bitter that loss can seem. In this second Servant Song, the servant reveals that he has known his calling before and given himself to it, but his efforts have been in vain.

Of course, we all contend with regrets and losses, but there is something particularly bitter that accompanies the demise of something on which we had pinned our hopes. Lost callings need to be mourned, so it is good that the servant makes this declaration—an encouragement to us to give voice to our losses and sing our own songs of lament. This lamentation needs space and time. We must not hurry through the songbook without first giving our deep attention to the songs that begin and end in a minor key.

Yet, the servant's experience is also that, in time, some kind of beautiful resolution may emerge: 'Yet surely my cause is with the Lord' (v. 4) he sings. Even here, however, there is a toughness to what is being sung, a recognition that the fulfilment of the servant's calling may be seen only by God: 'my reward [is] with my God' (v. 4). This was van Gogh's experience in his own lifetime, for it was only after his death that the results of his dedication to his calling were recognised.

Reflection

What losses are you mourning at this time? Create some space today to sing (or write, draw or paint) a song of lament. Be curious about the possibility of something new emerging, a 'Yet surely…' moment.

Ian Adams

A shining light

I am honoured in the sight of the Lord, and my God has become my strength—he says, 'It is too light a thing that you should be my servant to raise up the tribes of Jacob and to restore the survivors of Israel; I will give you as a light to the nations, that my salvation may reach to the end of the earth.'

At this point, the scope of the Servant Song and its potential effects begin to widen. For those in exile hearing the song for the first time, its reach must have been surprising. It was hard enough to imagine that somehow there might be salvation for the subjugated Jewish people in Babylon and harder still to imagine how their release might somehow open up salvation for others—but this is the message. God's salvation—then and now—is not only for the tribes of Jacob and the people of Israel but also for all nations and all peoples!

Perhaps we can sense links here to what Jesus would teach some 500 years later when he referred to the coming kingdom of God, the kingdom of heaven on earth. Salvation is not just about the liberation of the individual from all that harms (although it is that) and not just about the liberation of people groups from oppression (although that, too, is included) but also about the healing of creation, a transformation of heart and speech and action that will truly reach to the ends of the earth.

So the reach of the Servant Song will be great, but it needs to be sung first of all where we are, in the usual mix of the day's events, in the mundane as well as in the dramatic. The light to the nations may begin, as it were, with something as simple as the lighting of a candle of welcome at a table. The salvation that reaches to the end of the earth may begin with a hand that reaches out to help others find (or keep) their feet.

Prayer

God of salvation, may the small actions I take around me today be an opening for your light to shine.

Ian Adams

ISAIAH 50:4 (NRSV)

Disciple and teacher, both

The Lord God has given me the tongue of a teacher, that I may know how to sustain the weary with a word. Morning by morning he wakens—wakens my ear to listen as those who are taught.

In the world of football, there is little more dramatic than a big knock-out match going to extra time and then possibly penalties. The teams' managers have just a few minutes on the pitch in which to gather their players around them and 'sustain the weary with a word' (v. 4). In the final minutes of normal time, the tired players may have begun to move away from long-planned tactics and started to fall back on their (undoubted) instinct, skill and passion. At this point, a good coach will know both what to say and how to say it to a group that are both team and individuals under pressure.

The opening for the third of the Servant Songs suggests that the servant must be both a teacher and a disciple. Some translations of this passage replace 'teacher' with 'disciple'—the word seems to allow for either or both meanings. Either way, perhaps the point is made well, that a good teacher must also always be a disciple and a good disciple must be open to being a teacher. That is because our learning is a continuous process. So, the youngest, newest disciple can, with humility, also teach from his or her own experience from day one.

You are a disciple. God's song of salvation is a gift for you today. It is yours to receive and yours to sing. If you allow it to do so, the song will bring you new energy, strength and purpose. You may also be a teacher! The way you live today in the spirit of Christ can be a gift to others around you so that you, too, can 'sustain the weary with a word' (v. 4).

Reflection

In the care of the Father, the Son and the Holy Spirit, may you be a disciple today—blessed with new energy, strength and purpose. May you also be a teacher—finding what you need to 'sustain the weary with a word' (v. 4).

IAN ADAMS

ISAIAH 50:5–7 (NRSV)

I will not hide my face

The Lord God has opened my ear, and I was not rebellious, I did not turn backward. I gave my back to those who struck me, and my cheeks to those who pulled out the beard; I did not hide my face from insult and spitting. The Lord God helps me.

I remember seeing a band play at a big festival in the late 1970s that did not meet the approval of a section of the crowd. Devo was an alternative rock band ahead of its time, and its attempts to play innovative music were met with showers of abuse and bottles. I cannot remember if the band cut the set short, but I still remember the unpleasant atmosphere that had been created by the abusers. Sometimes the song is not well received.

In the passage today, we are reminded that sometimes the Song of God's Servant will not be well received. A commitment to worship the Lord God in the time of the Jewish Exile was not going to be popular with everyone. A decision to follow the path of Jesus is not going to be universally popular now. Of course, we like it when we are well received and when Christ's people follow his way with love and humility, they will often be met with welcome and thanks… but not always.

In such cases, how do we respond? A low profile might possibly seem the most sensible option, but the servant in this third song suggests that we consider another way. Faced with abuse and opposition, he does not hide his face but looks the abuser in the eye, offering himself for whatever may come his way, refusing to return abuse for abuse.

We may now find ourselves here thinking of Jesus, who was calm (and at times silent) before his accusers. Sometimes the best way to face opposition may be to stand before it, trusting in the One in whose strength we are held, and saying to ourselves, 'I will not turn away, I will not hide my face.'

Reflection

Reflect on how you instinctively respond to criticism or opposition. Learning from the servant, could there be another way?

IAN ADAMS

Authenticity and love

Who has believed what we have heard? And to whom has the arm of the Lord been revealed? For he grew up before him like a young plant, and like a root out of dry ground; he had no form or majesty that we should look at him, nothing in his appearance that we should desire him. He was despised and rejected by others; a man of suffering and acquainted with infirmity; and as one from whom others hide their faces he was despised, and we held him of no account.

The singers in reality TV singing competitions gradually sharpen their image (or perhaps more accurately have their image sharpened) over the course of the competition. It seems that we like our heroes to look the part! In the fourth of the Servant Songs, more details begin to emerge about the image, character and nature of the servant. It is clear that this servant will come as a surprise, even as a shock to many: 'Who has believed what we have heard? And to whom has the arm of the Lord been revealed?' (v. 1).

Some think that one of the origins of the Servant in the Songs may lie in the story of a person suffering from leprosy. This would fit well with the description of 'a man of suffering and acquainted with infirmity; and as one from whom others hide their faces' (v. 3). At the very least we might say that the servant is visibly unimpressive—a weed breaking through arid soil.

How interesting that God's salvation will be sung into being by one we could all too easily dismiss as irrelevant or untouchable. A reminder, surely, that we need to learn to see people as God sees them. A reminder, too, that our own disfigurements in life do not preclude us from being called or able to sing God's song of salvation. In fact, might it be possible that our disfigurements are the very experiences that qualify us to sing the Christ song with authenticity and love?

Prayer

God help me, I pray, to see my disfigurements as the very place from which your song may be sung today.

Ian Adams

Into silence

All we like sheep have gone astray; we have all turned to our own way, and the Lord has laid on him the iniquity of us all. He was oppressed, and he was afflicted, yet he did not open his mouth; like a lamb that is led to the slaughter, and like a sheep that before its shearers is silent, so he did not open his mouth.

Today we fall into silence—our own silence and the silence of God.

Sometimes, faced with the truth of our own actions (or inactions), all we can do is fall silent. The truth is that we have all 'gone astray' (v. 6). Certainly some of the bad stuff we have experienced has been done to us, but we will surely recognise there are some unhealthy paths we have chosen and that is down to us. No one else can be blamed for those things; they represent 'our own way' (v. 6).

Now, there is a strong argument to be made that, as Church, we have at times overdone our emphasis on sin, causing damage which has far exceeded the possibility of promised salvation. With that as a very important precursor, this Servant Song passage suggests, nevertheless, sometimes it is healthy for us to recognise and accept our own complicity—to fall into silence.

This Servant Song does not end there. In the sacrificial metaphor so familiar to YHWH's people, 'the Lord has laid on him [the servant] the iniquity of us all' (v. 6). What's particularly interesting here is the silence of the servant. Unlike us—who often tend to wriggle and protest and deny our part in what has gone wrong—the servant accepts the wrongdoing of others in silence. In this silence comes salvation.

One of the most famous works of the 20th-century American classical composer John Cage is entitled 4' 33" and is commonly spoken of as being four and a half minutes of silence. In fact, Cage's intention seems to have been for the surprising silence to enable the sounds in which music is, of course, made to be heard. Either way, interesting things happen in silence.

Reflection

Sit (or stand, walk, run, swim or cycle) in silence for 4 minutes and 33 seconds.

Ian Adams

We are prayed for

The righteous one, my servant, shall make many righteous, and he shall bear their iniquities. Therefore I will allot him a portion with the great, and he shall divide the spoil with the strong; because he poured out himself to death, and was numbered with the transgressors; yet he bore the sin of many, and made intercession for the transgressors.

Can the actions of one single person or group make a difference? In a tough world it is easy to imagine that they could not. How can we possibly make a difference for good? This must have been a particular challenge for the Jewish community exiled in Babylon in the sixth century BC. How could this oppressed community bring about salvation for anyone, never mind for themselves?

In today's passage, at the close of the fourth Servant Song, we hear the voice of God declaring that one can make a difference. In fact, this particular one—the servant—will change everything. His righteousness will make many righteous. His bearing of the iniquities of others will release them from those iniquities. Maybe the exiles themselves can make a difference after all, and/or perhaps there is one in their line who will do so.

Here, of course, we pick up resonances with the gospel story of the sacrificial death of the righteous Jesus for the world. In a memorable phrase—'he poured out himself to death' (v. 12)—we glimpse something of what this cost him, yet he chose to continue: 'yet he bore the sin of many' (v. 12).

There's a further tantalising connection in this passage with the ongoing nature and work of Jesus. In the Servant Song, Isaiah has God declaring that the servant 'made intercession for the transgressors' (v. 12). Some 600 years later, the writer of a letter to some early Jewish followers of Jesus was to encourage them by writing that, now and always, Jesus is praying for them (Hebrews 7:25). Within the life of God, we are prayed for! What encouragement as we ask how on earth we might make a difference?

Prayer

Jesus, for your prayers for me, for us, for the world, I thank you.

IAN ADAMS

A calling, a manifesto

> The spirit of the Lord God is upon me, because the Lord has anointed me; he has sent me to bring good news to the oppressed, to bind up the broken-hearted, to proclaim liberty to the captives, and release to the prisoners.

In the final few days of notes on the Servant Songs, we spend time now with a passage that is possibly another Servant Song or at least is clearly in tune with the spirit of them. It is the opening of chapter 61, part of Trito-Isaiah and probably composed after the homecoming of the Jewish people from exile.

Here, the prophet Isaiah sets out what he can see is beginning to happen as well as what he can imagine coming into being in and around a people restored. The Servant Songs are ending on a new note of confidence. The healing has begun—and its freeing effects will be experienced far and wide.

This is, of course, a pivotal passage for the story of Jesus, too. At the start of his public ministry, he stands to read in the synagogue at Nazareth, his home town, and the scroll of the prophet Isaiah is handed to him. He unfurls the scroll, pauses at this passage, then begins to read: 'The Spirit of the Lord God is upon me' (Luke 4:16–20). The passage has deep personal meaning for him, and everyone present senses that something truly important is occurring.

In choosing these words, Jesus announces that the Messiah has come. It is both a declaration of his calling and also a manifesto for change, articulating an agenda for the will of God for the world: good news for the oppressed, binding up for the broken-hearted, liberty for all those in captivity, release for all who are imprisoned. The Servant Song continues to be sung and it must surely be sung by us, as it was sung by Jesus and by Isaiah.

Reflection

Imagine this passage as containing the principles that could form a manifesto or agenda for how you could help to bring change for good in God's name where you are today. How would you express this in your own words and your own setting?

IAN ADAMS

The vengeance of forgiveness

To proclaim the year of the Lord 's favour, and the day of venge-ance of our God; to comfort all who mourn; to provide for those who mourn in Zion—to give them a garland instead of ashes, the oil of gladness instead of mourning, the mantle of praise instead of a faint spirit.

The Servant Song manifesto continues to unfold. Immediately, though, there is a difficulty for us. Up to this point, the manifesto has been posi-tive, and it continues in that vein with the beautiful calling that we have here to 'proclaim the year of the Lord's favour', but the next part may well make us uncomfortable—the idea of vengeance.

Of course, for a people who have been long oppressed, the possibil-ity of vengeance on those who have perpetrated their oppression seems both right and natural. We, too, know how satisfying it is to see a film in which the baddies get their comeuppance. Instinctively, however, we also know that the gospel does not work like that. It is precisely not about comeuppance, but lifting up. So how are we to sing this song of God's vengeance?

Perhaps the first thing to note is that any vengeance is God's. It must not come from our desire for retribution but from the depths of God's justice and love. Could God's vengeance be the surprising victory of something unexpected? Not the traditional retribution of just deserts, but a very different type of vengeance—the vengeance of comfort for the oppressed and forgiveness for the oppressor? A vengeance that ushers in a cycle of peace?

Here we sense traces of the hope that will, hundreds of years later in Jesus, produce the Beatitudes. Where we have only been left with ashes, there will be garlands. As it says here, where there has been mourning, the oil of gladness will pour again and the faintest of spirits will be lifted in hope. That is an unexpected but most welcome kind of vengeance.

Reflection

For what are you seeking vengeance? How might this passage reshape what you are hoping to see?

Ian Adams

Become like an oak

They will be called oaks of righteousness, the planting of the Lord, to display his glory. They shall build up the ancient ruins, they shall raise up the former devastations; they shall repair the ruined cities, the devastations of many generations.

Become like a tree, but not just any tree, be like an oak! In the poetic wisdom of Isaiah, we close this series of notes with a memorable metaphor for how we may live today—as 'oaks of righteousness' (v. 3).

The oak is a tree of great resilience, strength and beauty and it usually seems to stand well in its setting, offering shade and hospitality to all the creatures around it. For those of us who live in a part of the world where the oak is native, it seems to carry something of the wisdom and story of the local landscape and its people.

For perhaps all of these reasons the wood of the oak is as valued now as it was in the time of Jesus, the carpenter's son, as a wonderful material with which to build, work, live, grow old and pass on to following generations. Perhaps Isaiah has this esteem for the oak in mind as he begins to imagine what the newly restored exiles might be capable of. Previously powerless under the oppressive rule of the Babylonian empire, they will now find the strength and imagination to 'build up the ancient ruins, they shall raise up the former devastations; they shall repair the ruined cities' (v. 4). Jerusalem's glory will be restored.

These oaks of rebuilding are not random but 'the planting of the Lord' (v. 3). This, Isaiah seems to be suggesting, is now the people's divinely given purpose. This rebuilding work is now their calling. Of course, every time and every place, every group and every society has its rebuilding challenges. What might be the rebuilding that you are being called to prepare for, begin or continue?

Blessing

In your imagination, can you see a building rising up from the ruins? What do you see? May you become 'oaks of righteousness' (v. 3). May you sense God's calling to rebuild, raise up and repair so may you know and share God's blessing.

IAN ADAMS

The shepherd and the lamb:
John 10—11

Confession time: John is not my favourite Gospel (that would be Luke). I find it at times overly spiritualised and prefer the down-to-earth approach of Mark and Luke or the Jewish flavour of Matthew. I was only reconciled to John when I saw the fantastic Riding Lights Theatre's dramatisation of it, which I have watched twice. Suddenly, the Jesus of John came alive for me and I liked him a lot better.

What I do love in John, however, is the seven great 'I am' sayings of Jesus, some of which are engraved on the beautiful 'Tablets of the Word' in Coventry Cathedral. There are also some great stories of women, such as the Samaritan woman at the well and, of course, Mary and Martha. In chapters 10 and 11 we have both—Jesus saying 'I am the good shepherd' and the extraordinary story of the raising of Lazarus, Martha and Mary's brother.

Although these chapters are less than halfway through the Gospel, the shadow of the cross is already looming large in them. Jesus tells his disciples, 'The good shepherd lays down his life for the sheep' (10:11). None of them could have understood at this point what this meant, but he is preparing them for what will be a great shock for all of them—what will, in fact, look like the end of all they had been hoping for.

In John 10 and 11 we meet a Jesus who cares for each of his followers individually, who calls us 'friends' and, in order to give life to us, is willing to sacrifice his own. We find a Jesus who not only tells but also shows us that the life of God is not defeated by death, but springs up anew wherever there is sorrow or need. We hear a call to be as self-sacrificing as him whenever God asks us to give up our own needs and wants for God's purposes. This is not because God enjoys putting us through difficulties, but because, under the law of the Spirit, it is always death—not necessarily literal death, but the thousand 'little deaths' we go through every day—that is the gate to life.

Veronica Zundel

We follow the good shepherd

'Very truly, I tell you, anyone who does not enter the sheepfold by the gate but climbs in by another way is a thief and a bandit. The one who enters by the gate is the shepherd of the sheep. The gatekeeper opens the gate for him, and the sheep hear his voice. He calls his own sheep by name and leads them out. When he has brought out all his own, he goes ahead of them, and the sheep follow him because they know his voice. They will not follow a stranger, but they will run from him because they do not know the voice of strangers.'

Have you ever watched the TV programme *One Man and his Dog*? It is hard to believe that watching a shepherd using a dog to herd sheep can be so fascinating and relaxing. Shepherds in Jesus' day did not use dogs, but managed their sheep by the sound of their own voice. As their master's voice became familiar to the sheep, they would follow its commands and go where they were told to.

Verse 1 has often been used to tell people they cannot come to God by following other religions. This is a misuse of its message. In its context, it clearly refers not to 'sheep' trying to get in by the back door, but 'shepherds' who do not know the sheep and, consequently, lead them astray. The first hearers of this parable would have been very familiar with 'sheep' standing for the people of Israel and 'shepherds' for their political and religious leaders (see, for example, Ezekiel 34:1–10).

How can we translate this into our own modern context? Sheep farmers still exist, although they are not a daily sight unless you live in a sheep-farming area, but we can still use this image to think about our spiritual leaders and maybe even our political ones. We may then apply this to any of our would-be leaders and ask, 'Does this person's theology, or policies, accord with the teaching of Jesus?' If not, they may be 'a thief and a bandit', seeking to profit from power rather than lead the sheep to good pasture.

Reflection

Where do you find 'pasture' for your soul? What 'feeds' you spiritually?

Veronica Zundel

In and out

So again Jesus said to them, 'Very truly, I tell you, I am the gate for the sheep. All who came before me are thieves and bandits; but the sheep did not listen to them. I am the gate. Whoever enters by me will be saved, and will come in and go out and find pasture. The thief comes only to steal and kill and destroy. I came that they may have life, and have it abundantly.'

Many years ago, the writer Brian Sibley scripted a radio programme called *The Door*, in which he examined the theme of doors in literature and faith. I am sure we can all think of examples—doors leading to unexpected places, doors locking people in or out or on which a sinister knock comes in the night.

In some translations Jesus calls himself 'the door' rather than 'the gate' (v. 7). Either way, his image changes from the shepherd who leads to the entrance that invites. We may knock on many doors in our lives, but Jesus tells his disciples that he is the only way to true security. This is not about going into a sheepfold and staying there. Sheep need grass, and the gate of the sheepfold is there to let the sheep out in the day as well as to shut them in safely at night.

If we see our faith only as a source of security, we will be of little use in the world—God's world, which is destined to be transformed in the kingdom of God. Jesus promises that his sheep 'will come in and go out' (v. 9): we are meant to venture out into the daily challenges of life as well as coming home to the security of our church or our personal prayers. Interestingly, 'pasture' is found outside the sheep pen, not just inside it. Though worship feeds us inwardly, we will find spiritual food in our Monday to Saturday lives, too, if we look for it. This is God's creation and God has hidden in it many things that are for our good.

Reflection

'The Lord will keep your going out and your coming in from this time on and for evermore' (Psalm 121:8).

VERONICA ZUNDEL

Knowing me, knowing you

'I am the good shepherd. The good shepherd lays down his life for the sheep. The hired hand, who is not the shepherd and does not own the sheep, sees the wolf coming and leaves the sheep and runs away—and the wolf snatches them and scatters them. The hired hand runs away because a hired hand does not care for the sheep. I am the good shepherd. I know my own and my own know me, just as the Father knows me and I know the Father. And I lay down my life for the sheep.'

For a long time I found it hard to believe that God really understood what it meant to me to be a woman—the physical experiences or social disadvantages that women encounter in a world that is still unequal. My image of God was too masculine and Jesus was a man, so how could he understand women's experiences?

This passage, however, tells us that 'I know my own and my own know me' (v. 14). Is it too hard to believe that Jesus knows us even better than we know ourselves? I struggle with this daily, but I also encounter many little incidents in my life that tell me God knows me very well, knows what I need and what I am capable of coping with. As a mother, while I have known my son since before he was born, I also know that parts of his personality and thoughts are a mystery. There is no mystery for God, however: God knows my son and me through and through.

What does this say to those of us who have a leadership role or pastoral responsibility in our churches? I think it tells us that we cannot minister in a Christlike way to our fellow Christians unless we really know them. Being in a very small church, I have the advantage of knowing its long-term members almost as well as I know my family, but larger congregations also need to gather in smaller groups where they can share deeply and support each other in their walk with Jesus.

Prayer

*Pray for those who are lonely even in church,
that others will welcome them.*

VERONICA ZUNDEL

Fling wide the gates

'I have other sheep that do not belong to this fold. I must bring them also, and they will listen to my voice. So there will be one flock, one shepherd. For this reason the Father loves me, because I lay down my life in order to take it up again. No one takes it from me, but I lay it down of my own accord. I have power to lay it down, and I have power to take it up again. I have received this command from my Father.'

Who is in and who is out? There was a time, as Matthew 15:24 shows, when Jesus declared that his mission was only to the Jewish people. A Gentile woman convinced him otherwise (Mark 7:24–30). As a human being who had emptied himself of divine status, he had to learn as he went about his work. This inclusive call was a lesson the early church struggled to learn, too, as the Council at Jerusalem in Acts 15 bears witness. Human beings have a recurrent tendency to form 'in-groups' from which others are excluded.

So here, in John, Jesus warns his disciples that, in following him, they are not joining an exclusive club. Casting the net wider is going to cause problems as people will have different cultures, different experiences, different opinions. It will be hard at times to discern what is of God and what habits or customs need to be left behind. As Christians, we have often got it wrong, wanting to exclude those whom God includes or thinking that, when people follow Jesus, they also have to follow Western culture (ironic, really, as the Christian faith originates from the Middle East!).

What relation does this have to Jesus talking about laying down his life and taking it up again? Well, I suspect that welcoming the stranger may require a 'laying down' of many ideas and practices we are attached to, but are not actually essential. We need the Spirit's power to do this 'dying', but, if we do, we will also find new life.

Reflection

'Open to me the gates of righteousness, that I may enter through them and give thanks to the Lord' (Psalm 118:19).

VERONICA ZUNDEL

81

Believe what you see

At that time the festival of the Dedication took place in Jerusalem. It was winter, and Jesus was walking in the temple, in the portico of Solomon. So the Jews gathered around him and said to him, 'How long will you keep us in suspense? If you are the Messiah, tell us plainly.' Jesus answered, 'I have told you, and you do not believe. The works that I do in my Father's name testify to me; but you do not believe, because you do not belong to my sheep. My sheep hear my voice. I know them, and they follow me. I give them eternal life, and they will never perish. No one will snatch them out of my hand. What my Father has given me is greater than all else, and no one can snatch it out of the Father's hand. The Father and I are one.'

Every winter, practising Jews celebrate Hanukkah, the feast of lights—what is called the Dedication above. It commemorates the rededication of the temple, in about 165BC, after it had been defiled by the pagan emperor.

Jesus goes to the temple to celebrate, but he does not just worship privately, he walks around the temple porticoes. Why? To admire the architecture? No: he predicted that 'not one stone will be left here upon another' (Matthew 24:2); the whole system of temple worship will be destroyed. Is he, then, reflecting on the destruction to come or the 'new temple' of 'living stones' that he will build with the lives of his disciples (1 Peter 2:4)? Perhaps, like the shepherd who leads the sheep out as well as in, he is making himself available to others who may want to question him—and they do.

To the Jewish leaders, however, he will not give a straight answer, pointing instead to the evidence of both his works and those who follow him. If his questioners cannot see God in what he does and in his disciples, they will never see God at all. To see Jesus is to see God.

Prayer

Father, help me to open my life to others and live in such a way that my life points to God.

VERONICA ZUNDEL

Rough justice

The Jews took up stones again to stone him. Jesus replied, 'I have shown you many good works from the Father. For which of these are you going to stone me?' The Jews answered, 'It is not for a good work that we are going to stone you, but for blasphemy, because you, though only a human being, are making yourself God.' Jesus answered, 'Is it not written in your law, "I said, you are gods"? If those to whom the word of God came were called "gods"... can you say that the one whom the Father has sanctified and sent into the world is blaspheming because I said, "I am God's Son"? If I am not doing the works of my Father, then do not believe me. But if I do them, even though you do not believe me, believe the works, so that you may know and understand that the Father is in me and I am in the Father.'

'No good deed goes unpunished', goes a cynical saying. Jesus' ironic question echoes this. Which of his miracles merits death? (Remember that when John says 'the Jews', he means the religious leaders of the time: sadly, this phrase has been used to fuel anti-Semitism.)

The apostle Peter tells us to 'accept the authority of every human institution... as sent by him to punish those who do wrong and to praise those who do right' (1 Peter 2:13), but sometimes authorities punish those who do right and praise those who do wrong. Only recently, the preacher at my church was a man who had been tried for obstructing the entrance to an arms fair, where illegal torture equipment was on sale. He was acquitted, thankfully, but the illegal arms sellers were not prosecuted!

In an unjust world, followers of Jesus should be getting into trouble. If we fear this, we have Jesus' affirmation that we have an innate power and dignity as human beings—so much so that scripture calls us 'gods'. This should give us courage to dissent from the world.

Reflection

'What are human beings that you are mindful of them, mortals that you care for them? Yet you have made them a little lower than God'
(Psalm 8:4–5).

VERONICA ZUNDEL

Home and away

Then they tried to arrest him again, but he escaped from their hands. He went away again across the Jordan to the place where John had been baptising earlier, and he remained there. Many came to him, and they were saying, 'John performed no sign, but everything that John said about this man was true.' And many believed in him there.

The Anabaptist tradition has had many groups that have chosen to withdraw from the world into their own communities—the Amish, Hutterites and conservative Mennonites. One reason may have been fear of further persecution in the countries to which they had fled, another, the desire to be free to practise their own culture and remain 'unstained by the world' (James 1:27). They were often known as 'the quiet in the land'.

There are times when we all need to dissociate ourselves from the world around us, to go to a quiet place for refreshment or discuss our next action. Here, Jesus escapes from Jerusalem and retreats to the Jordan, where his ministry began. (How did he manage to slip away from his would-be arresters? Did he have help from his disciples or was it just the force of his personality?)

We know, however, that he will return to Jerusalem to meet his fate. If we live only in a 'Christian bubble'—going to church meetings, listening to Christian music, reading Christian books, keeping away from any event where we might be challenged—how will the rest of the world see what it means to follow Jesus? Like the sheep that the shepherd calls home and leads out again, we must get involved with the contemporary world. It is the only way we can witness to our faith and participate in building the kingdom of God.

The Amish and their radical way of life have become well known lately, not only because of the many (sometimes exploitative) television programmes about them but also following on from their amazing forgiveness when a school shooting happened in their community. If we are distinctive, the world will sometimes come to us.

Reflection

What am I, or my church, called to at the moment:
to rest and regroup or venture out?

VERONICA ZUNDEL

The absence of God

Now a certain man was ill, Lazarus of Bethany, the village of Mary and her sister Martha. Mary was the one who anointed the Lord with perfume and wiped his feet with her hair; her brother Lazarus was ill. So the sisters sent a message to Jesus, 'Lord, he whom you love is ill.' But when Jesus heard it, he said, 'This illness does not lead to death; rather it is for God's glory, so that the Son of God may be glorified through it.' Accordingly, though Jesus loved Martha and her sister and Lazarus, after having heard that Lazarus was ill, he stayed two days longer in the place where he was.

I have just read an online post that says, in effect, 'I don't think God cares about me at all.' Most of us have felt like that at some time. So what should we think or do when God appears to be deaf to our prayers, however long we have prayed them for; those times when God simply seems to be absent? It is a question to which there is no simple answer.

What, then, do we make of a Jesus who, when he hears one of his closest friends is ill and he has the power of healing, chooses to stay away? What impression will the disciples have formed—that he no longer loves Lazarus, has run out of compassion or is scared of going near Jerusalem again?

Why did Jesus do it? Was he testing his followers' faith or that of Lazarus and his sisters? Did he actually not know why—just that this was what God asked him to do and he and his disciples had to trust it was right?

Sometimes I think that faith is like learning to ride a bicycle. When you start, your dad or big sister holds on to the seat or the handlebars and helps you balance. Later, as you grow more confident, they take their hand away. That is the scariest part, when you no longer feel their support. Yet, if they do not do this, you will never learn to ride.

Prayer
Absent God, help me to stay present to you till I feel your presence again.

VERONICA ZUNDEL

Facing the worst

Then after this he said to the disciples, 'Let us go to Judea again.' The disciples said to him, 'Rabbi, the Jews were just now trying to stone you, and are you going there again?' Jesus answered, 'Are there not twelve hours of daylight? Those who walk during the day do not stumble, because they see the light of this world. But those who walk at night stumble, because the light is not in them.' After saying this, he told them, 'Our friend Lazarus has fallen asleep, but I am going there to awaken him.' The disciples said to him, 'Lord, if he has fallen asleep, he will be all right.'... Then Jesus told them plainly, 'Lazarus is dead. For your sake I am glad I was not there, so that you may believe. But let us go to him.' Thomas, who was called the Twin, said to his fellow disciples, 'Let us also go, that we may die with him.'

My husband deals with any challenging situations by asking, 'What's the worst that could happen?' It helps him, but does not really work for me. The disciples sound quite like my husband as they are ready to contemplate the dangers of a return to Judaea. Their conclusion, however, is not to take the risk, but stay put. All except Thomas.

I think we do Thomas a disservice in labelling him 'Doubting Thomas'. Rather, he is apt to doubt good news—the resurrection. When it comes to bad news, however, he is all too ready to believe it. You cannot fault his commitment. He is willing to follow Jesus to the death. Are we? After all, that is what discipleship really is—a willingness to die for Jesus or our Christian sisters and brothers: 'Do you not know that all of us who have been baptised into Christ Jesus were baptised into his death?' (Romans 6:3).

In one of those paradoxes God delights in, Thomas' and Jesus' willingness to risk death will be the route to new life for Lazarus.

Reflection

'We have been buried with him by baptism into death, so that, just as Christ was raised from the dead by the glory of the Father, so we too might walk in newness of life' (Romans 6:4).

VERONICA ZUNDEL

Hard to believe

When Jesus arrived, he found that Lazarus had already been in the tomb for four days... When Martha heard that Jesus was coming, she went and met him, while Mary stayed at home. Martha said to Jesus, 'Lord, if you had been here, my brother would not have died. But even now I know that God will give you whatever you ask of him.' Jesus said to her, 'Your brother will rise again.' Martha said to him, 'I know that he will rise again in the resurrection on the last day.' Jesus said to her, 'I am the resurrection and the life. Those who believe in me, even though they die, will live.... Do you believe this?' She said to him, 'Yes, Lord, I believe that you are the Messiah, the Son of God, the one coming into the world.'

The amazing story of Lazarus is especially close to my heart as I, too, lost an only brother, by his own hand, when I was 22 and he was 27. 'Your brother will rise again' comes to me as a personal promise and, though my brother was not a Christian, I trust in God's great compassion for a very troubled soul.

Martha does what we all need to do when disaster strikes: she searches for Jesus. The sisters had many friends around, but the friend she needs most is him. Mary is too upset even to come to him, but he will come to her.

It is hard to believe in resurrection. Martha quite understandably misreads what Jesus says, thinking he is talking about the final resurrection, but Jesus is offering more than she can imagine. What she is willing to affirm is that she believes in Jesus as the human face of God, as God with us (John 1:14).

For most of us, there are probably doctrines that we find hard to swallow. In some cases, they are not biblical, so we do not need to believe them. In others, they are just hard to understand. All God really requires of us is that we trust and follow Jesus.

Reflection

'Everyone who believes that Jesus is the Christ has been born of God'
(1 John 5:1).

VERONICA ZUNDEL

Weeping with those who weep

When [Martha] had said this, she went back and called her sister Mary, and told her privately, 'The Teacher is here and is calling for you.' And when she heard it, she got up quickly and went to him... The Jews who were with her in the house, consoling her, saw Mary get up quickly and go out. They followed her because they thought that she was going to the tomb to weep there. When Mary came where Jesus was and saw him, she knelt at his feet and said to him, 'Lord, if you had been here, my brother would not have died.' When Jesus saw her weeping, and the Jews who came with her also weeping, he was greatly disturbed in spirit and deeply moved. He said, 'Where have you laid him?' They said to him, 'Lord, come and see.' Jesus began to weep. So the Jews said, 'See how he loved him!' But some of them said, 'Could not he who opened the eyes of the blind man have kept this man from dying?'

After a death, especially a premature death, those left behind often keep repeating the same perplexed statements. 'If only that doctor had come sooner', 'If only she had been able to kick her drug habit', 'If only we had known how he felt'. Mary's anguished cry is the same as Martha's: 'Lord, if you had been here' (v. 21). When the worst happens, we may think that all hope has died. How can life go on without our child, brother, mother?

Jesus knows he is about to perform an incredible miracle, yet still he feels the pain of loss. The Greek word translated as 'deeply moved' literally means something like 'his guts were wrenched'. This is profound human emotion; Jesus was not some sort of divine Superman. The sentence given four words in the version of the passage above for verse 35 is rendered in other versions with just two: 'Jesus wept'.

Death is not a blessed release. It is a fierce foe, a consequence of the fall, our 'last enemy'. Jesus weeps at it and he joins in our weeping.

Reflection and prayer

'For he must reign until he has put all his enemies under his feet. The last enemy to be destroyed is death' (1 Corinthians 15:25–26).
Lord, help me believe this.

VERONICA ZUNDEL

You want me to do what?

Then Jesus, again greatly disturbed, came to the tomb. It was a cave, and a stone was lying against it. Jesus said, 'Take away the stone.' Martha, the sister of the dead man, said to him, 'Lord, already there is a stench because he has been dead for four days.' Jesus said to her, 'Did I not tell you that if you believed, you would see the glory of God?' So they took away the stone. And Jesus looked upward and said, 'Father, I thank you for having heard me. I knew that you always hear me, but I have said this for the sake of the crowd standing here, so that they may believe that you sent me.' When he had said this, he cried with a loud voice, 'Lazarus, come out!' The dead man came out, his hands and feet bound with strips of cloth, and his face wrapped in a cloth. Jesus said to them, 'Unbind him, and let him go.'

It is not that Martha does not have faith. Indeed, she has already declared her trust in Jesus, in similar words to those Peter used at Caesarea Philippi (Matthew 16:16): 'You are the Messiah, the son of the living God.' It is just that she is the practical type, so she is thinking, 'You do not open a grave that has been occupied for the best part of a week, especially in a hot country.' Who wants to see the rotting corpse of their late brother?

I am often in Martha's position. I look at a situation that needs God's intervention and think, 'It probably will not get any better because things like that just don't happen.' Yet we can all probably name events in our lives that we thought would never happen, situations we thought would never change, but they did. When we cease to expect surprises from God, we essentially cease to have faith. In fact, that could be a definition of faith: expecting surprises from God.

The implicit subtext of this story is obedience. The friends obey the command to remove the stone and Lazarus obeys the call to come out. Without this, the miracle could not happen.

Reflection

In what way has God said to you, or is God saying to you,
'[Your name], come out!'?

VERONICA ZUNDEL

Inconvenient faith

Many of the Jews therefore, who had come with Mary and had seen what Jesus did, believed in him. But some of them went to the Pharisees and told them what he had done. So the chief priests and the Pharisees called a meeting of the council, and said, 'What are we to do? This man is performing many signs. If we let him go on like this, everyone will believe in him, and the Romans will come and destroy both our holy place and our nation.'

We have had some incidents in the UK recently of Christians portraying themselves as 'persecuted'. Maybe there has been a little discrimination, but we can hardly compare our situation, in a country where bishops sit in the legislature, to places where Christians are imprisoned or executed for acting in accordance with their faith. Such places are many: more Christians are killed worldwide than any other faith group.

If we live out the implications of Jesus' call to us, we will not be popular. Our faith may lead us to protest against governments or big corporations, care for those whom society rejects and (as the Quakers say) 'speak truth to power'. So, the people who report the raising of Lazarus to their religious leaders are right to perceive that this sort of faith is a threat to established power. We cannot have God doing things that are not sanctioned by the religious authorities!

In his book *Money, Sex and Power*, Richard Foster wrote about the three classic temptations that are addressed by the monastic vows of poverty, chastity and obedience. I sometimes wonder if power is not the most harmful and the most insidious. Scandals involving financial corruption or sexual misbehaviour tend to come out and be punished, but abuse of power can be subtle, almost invisible. The only safe way to exercise power is to surrender it, not by capitulating to others, but becoming a servant, as Jesus did. The Pharisees wanted to hold on to what little power they had, but, for Jesus, the power shown in raising Lazarus led to the powerlessness of the cross.

Prayer

Servant King, if I have power, in church, work or family,
help me to use it sacrificially.

VERONICA ZUNDEL

God in unexpected places

But one of them, Caiaphas, who was high priest that year, said to [the council], 'You know nothing at all! You do not understand that it is better for you to have one man die for the people than to have the whole nation destroyed.' He did not say this on his own, but being high priest that year he prophesied that Jesus was about to die for the nation, and not for the nation only, but to gather into one the dispersed children of God. So from that day on they planned to put him to death. Jesus therefore no longer walked about openly among the Jews, but went from there to a town called Ephraim in the region near the wilderness; and he remained there with the disciples.

The other night I saw the very funny play *The God Particle* by James Cary, a Christian who writes for several TV comedies. In the play, strange things happen to a new vicar, including a donkey in a nearby field talking to him (he has been reading about Balaam, in Numbers 22).

God seems to delight in using unexpected speakers (even four-legged ones!). Here, too, God's choice is unexpected as he speaks through Caiaphas, who will engineer Jesus' death. How could a man who clearly does not recognise the presence of God in Jesus still speak the word and do the will of God? How can the tragedy of Jesus' crucifixion be good news?

This passage tells us two things. First, that God does not abandon those whom God calls. Caiaphas may have been blind to God doing a new thing, but, as the representative of the chosen people, he is still able to prophesy, though he does not understand the full implication of his words. God has not abandoned the Jewish people and will not abandon anyone who wants to do right.

Second, what looks like a total tragedy in our lives can still be a place of redemption. Violent death is always bad news, but the resurrection shows us that God can bring good out of the very worst.

Reflection

*'The stone that the builders rejected has become the chief cornerstone…
this was the Lord's doing, and it is amazing in our eyes'*
(Psalm 118:22; Matthew 21:42).

VERONICA ZUNDEL

A wanted man

Now the Passover of the Jews was near, and many went up from the country to Jerusalem before the Passover to purify themselves. They were looking for Jesus and were asking one another as they stood in the temple, 'What do you think? Surely he will not come to the festival, will he?' Now the chief priests and the Pharisees had given orders that anyone who knew where Jesus was should let them know, so that they might arrest him.

If this were a film, now is the moment the ominous music would kick in. The net is tightening and Jesus' arrest is imminent. It is appropriate that all this should happen at Passover, the feast commemorating one of the worst moments for the Jews, as well as their rescue from it, and, of course, the sacrifice of a lamb at Passover gives meaning to John the Baptist's title for Jesus—the Lamb of God.

There must have been many who knew where Jesus was, but only one, Judas, told the religious leaders. Keeping a secret can be hard, especially if you fear punishment for not telling. I receive mailings from 'Freedom from Torture' (formerly the Medical Foundation for Victims of Torture) and often see stories of people who were tortured in order to get names of other dissidents out of them, so I admire those who did not lead the authorities to Jesus.

We should not condemn Judas, though, just as the Bible does not: it simply relates his remorse and what happened to him. Like Caiaphas, he was unwittingly doing what God wanted and the Bible simply says he 'handed over' Jesus (John 18: 35). One way or another, Jesus' death had to happen.

What about us? Do we know where Jesus is? Is he in the churches or in the streets helping the homeless or in a toddler group where leaders seek to support vulnerable mothers or in government seeking to make just laws? Our command is not to keep his whereabouts secret but let people know where they can find him. I am not very good at this and I pray to be better at it.

Prayer

God of revelation, help me see where Jesus is and tell others.

VERONICA ZUNDEL

Misunderstanding the Bible

Some of the passages of scripture that we shall be looking at over the next fortnight are very popular and much loved. They can also be puzzling, however, and are frequently misunderstood. I hope that these notes will be genuinely helpful for *New Daylight* readers wrestling with parts of the Bible or even sayings of Jesus that are not easy to understand. My only intention will be to find in them, as best we can, what the heart of their message is for us today.

Some of them are words or sayings we may have found hard to understand or accept over the years. Others may be phrases or verses that we have known since childhood, but have never questioned or wondered about their deeper meaning. Let me start by saying, the apostle told his young apprentice Timothy to win God's approval by 'rightly explaining the word of truth' (2 Timothy 2:15). The Greek word used for 'explaining' literally means 'cutting straight' (hence, the 'dividing the word' of the King James Version). We might paraphrase it as 'getting to the heart of the meaning' and my hope is that, together, we may be able to do just that as we look at these particular passages of scripture.

This seems to me particularly important where the sayings of Jesus are concerned. At times he seems to speak almost brutally ('hate father and mother', Luke 14:26) or urge his followers to do things that seem inconsistent with his message of forgiveness and love: 'if your eye causes you to sin, tear it out' (Matthew 5:29). Our natural reaction is to skip over these apparently difficult sayings and stick with the ones we are comfortable with, but the truth is, Jesus of Nazareth was not 'comfortable'. He dealt with truth in the most blunt way, but always to heal, never to harm, even when his language seems incongruous to our modern ears.

So, I hope the next two weeks' notes will help all of us as we look at some of the really difficult—and apparently incongruous—parts of scripture we love and respect and on which our knowledge of God's truth depends. Our purpose, as always, is to shine 'new daylight' on the sacred texts.

David Winter

Eve, the 'helpmeet'?

Then the Lord God said, 'It is not good that the man should be alone; I will make him a helper as his partner.' So out of the ground the Lord God formed every animal of the field and every bird of the air... but for the man there was not found a helper as his partner. So the Lord God caused a deep sleep to fall upon the man, and he slept; then he took one of his ribs and closed up its place with flesh. And the rib that the Lord God had taken from the man he made into a woman and brought her to the man. Then the man said, 'This at last is bone of my bones and flesh of my flesh; this one shall be called Woman, for out of Man this one was taken.' Therefore a man leaves his father and his mother and clings to his wife, and they become one flesh.

To get to the heart of the opening chapters of Genesis, readers need a few clues and a lot of imagination. The first chapter is an account of creation that begins with God and is completed with the creating by him of human beings 'in his image': 'male and female he created them' (Genesis 1:27).

Chapter 2 conveys the same message, but in the form of a story—the garden of Eden, the human being formed from the dust and the creation of the multiplicity of birds and animals. Finally, the man, needing a suitable companion, is given one who is in every respect like him ('flesh of my flesh', 2:23) except for her gender. Now the human race is complete: man and woman, each made 'in the image of God' (1:27).

There is no suggestion of one being superior to the other. The woman was not created to be Adam's 'servant', but his partner: that is what the old word 'helpmeet' meant. Here we can see the first glimpses of the truth that would only be fully revealed in Christ, in whom 'there is no longer male and female; for all of you are one' (Galatians 3:28).

Reflection

It is 'in Christ' that men and women can become
all God intends them to be.

DAVID WINTER

Exodus 20:1–2, 4–7 (NRSV)

The holy name

Then God spoke all these words: I am the Lord your God, who brought you out of the land of Egypt, out of the house of slavery... You shall not make for yourself an idol, whether in the form of anything that is in heaven above, or that is on the earth beneath, or that is in the water under the earth. You shall not bow down to them or worship them; for I the Lord your God am a jealous God, punishing children for the iniquity of parents, to the third and the fourth generation of those who reject me, but showing steadfast love to the thousandth generation of those who love me and keep my commandments. You shall not make wrongful use of the name of the Lord your God, for the Lord will not acquit anyone who misuses his name.

There are two possible areas of misunderstanding in this passage. The first is the notion of punishment extended not simply to those who have practised 'iniquity' but also to three or four generations of their descendants. Does this mean that we can be punished for something our great-great-great-grandfather did?

The short answer is 'no'. Of course, the consequences of evil can profoundly affect succeeding generations, but only for 'those who reject me'. This is not a curse that would afflict the innocent children of evil-doers. Not only that, but God's mercy will extend much further, not merely to three or four generations but also the 'thousandth' generation of those who love him. He is 'jealous' only in the sense that they are his and only his.

The other possible misunderstanding is over taking God's holy name 'in vain', as the old translations say. The word translated 'in vain' really means 'wrongfully' or 'for evil ends'. God's name in Hebrew thought was his power, never to be invoked lightly or for our own ends. It is always, as Jesus prayed, 'not my will but yours be done' (Luke 22:42).

Reflection

Satan invited Jesus to manipulate the power of God by jumping off a pinnacle and claiming his promise of angelic intervention. 'Do not put the Lord your God to the test', Jesus countered (Luke 4:9–12).

DAVID WINTER

The God of hill and plain

I lift up my eyes to the hills—from where will my help come? My help comes from the Lord, who made heaven and earth. He will not let your foot be moved; he who keeps you will not slumber. He who keeps Israel will neither slumber nor sleep. The Lord is your keeper; the Lord is your shade at your right hand. The sun shall not strike you by day, nor the moon by night. The Lord will keep you from all evil; he will keep your life. The Lord will keep your going out and your coming in from this time on and for evermore.

The key to this passage is something that is not in the original text because the Hebrew language does not have question marks. Where does my help come from? The old translations suggest it comes from the hills ('from whence cometh my help'), but this is a question, not an answer. That is in the rest of the psalm: 'My help comes from the Lord, who made heaven and earth' (v. 2).

From earliest times, human beings had looked at the hills around them with awe. They stood as symbols of strength and beauty, reaching up into the sky. What more likely place to seek and find God? Many ancient cultures located the 'gods' on hilltops, including the Greeks, whose deities had their home on Mount Olympus.

The people of Israel, however, had to learn that God was not 'located' anywhere, whether in the valleys or the hills. Our help comes from the Lord who made 'heaven and earth' (literally; v. 2). The 'heaven and the highest heaven' cannot contain him, nor any earthly temple (1 Kings 8:27). We may feel spiritually uplifted on a mountaintop, but, in truth we are no nearer God there than if we were in a submarine. He is not the God of a place, but the God of everywhere. As Psalm 139 (vv. 7–10) asserts, there is simply nowhere we can go where he is not.

Reflection

The loving care of our God surrounds us everywhere: 'In his hand are the depths of the earth; the heights of the mountains are his also' (Psalm 95:4).

DAVID WINTER

Thinking about tomorrow

[Jesus said] 'Therefore do not worry, saying, "What will we eat?" or "What will we drink?" or "What will we wear?" For it is the Gentiles who strive for all these things; and indeed your heavenly Father knows that you need all these things. But strive first for the kingdom of God and his righteousness, and all these things will be given to you as well. So do not worry about tomorrow, for tomorrow will bring worries of its own. Today's trouble is enough for today.'

'Do not worry' has always seemed to me a rather pointless piece of advice, mainly because the recipient of the advice is worried already. There is no money to pay the rent. The doctor has just told us that we are seriously ill. The Christmas turkey has just turned to cinders in the oven. Of course we are 'worried'—it is only natural.

Yet, here we have Jesus, in a well-loved passage from the Sermon on the Mount, urging his disciples to not be 'anxious'. Do not worry, he says, about food or clothes or health—the very things we habitually worry about. Then he caps it with the secret worry that haunts our days, which is not what has happened, but what might happen: 'do not worry about tomorrow' (v. 34). We may not find his reason all that reassuring, either: 'for tomorrow will bring worries of its own' (v. 34)!

This whole passage (from verse 25) has to be read as a complete argument, hung on its key clause: 'But strive first for the kingdom of God' (v. 33). We worry when we put our own needs, desires, plans and wishes first. Reverse this practice, he recommends. Put God's will, his standards of righteousness and justice, his loving purpose first and then 'all these things will be given to you as well' (v. 33). Peace of mind and inner confidence do not come from money in the bank or a reassuring medical check-up, but from being at one with our Creator. Like most of the Sermon on the Mount, it is strong medicine. Jesus is setting demanding priorities and goals for his disciples—kingdom values for the people of the kingdom.

Reflection

We find here an absolute provision ('all these things', v. 33) for an absolute priority ('strive first', v. 33).

DAVID WINTER

Lead us not into temptation

[Jesus said] 'After this manner therefore pray ye: Our Father which art in heaven, Hallowed be thy name. Thy kingdom come. Thy will be done in earth, as it is in heaven. Give us this day our daily bread. And forgive us our debts, as we forgive our debtors. And lead us not into temptation, but deliver us from evil: For thine is the kingdom, and the power, and the glory, for ever. Amen. For if ye forgive men their trespasses, your heavenly Father will also forgive you.'

Although we can now use the Lord's Prayer in other translations, this one, using the word 'trespasses' instead of 'debts', is probably still the best-known version. Apart from the odd-sounding 'which' at the start (God is not a thing, but a person), its message is clear enough and its language still familiar to many people. Judging by Jesus' comment following the 'Amen' of the prayer, he was most keen that his disciples should take note of how the process of forgiveness works: God forgives, we forgive.

The major problem in terms of misunderstanding is the last petition: 'lead us not into temptation' (v. 13). I remember the vicar raising this at my confirmation class over 70 years ago, asking, 'How can we think of God "leading us into temptation"?' Did James (1:13–14, NRSV) not make it very clear, 'No one, when tempted, should say, "I am being tempted by God"; for God cannot be tempted by evil and he himself tempts no one'?

There is a simple correction that removes this problem, but, when it has been proposed, most people have disliked it: 'do not bring us to the time of trial'. It is what the prayer actually says, but familiarity has won over accuracy.

The word translated 'temptation' means, in context, 'testing'. God can put us to the test, but he does not tempt us to do what is wrong. As James also says, that is entirely our own doing!

Reflection

'God is faithful, and he will not let you be tested beyond your strength, but with the testing he will also provide the way out so that you may be able to endure it' (1 Corinthians 10:13).

DAVID WINTER

Mutilation unnecessary

[Jesus said] 'You have heard that it was said, "You shall not commit adultery." But I say to you that everyone who looks at a woman with lust has already committed adultery with her in his heart. If your right eye causes you to sin, tear it out and throw it away; it is better for you to lose one of your members than for your whole body to be thrown into hell. And if your right hand causes you to sin, cut it off and throw it away; it is better for you to lose one of your members than for your whole body to go into hell.'

The first section of the Sermon on the Mount, of which today's passage is a part, finds Jesus taking the law of Moses, which the people knew well, and pushing it to its ultimate challenge. Do not kill? Not good enough: do not be angry. Love your neighbour? Not good enough: love your enemy. Do not commit adultery? Not good enough: reject lustful longings. It seems Jesus wanted to show that the zealous teachers of the Law, who knew all the pettifogging rules and were proud of the way they observed them, were failing to recognise their true implication. The law of God is about holiness rather than keeping rules.

Jesus then embarks on a daring use of hyperbole—that kind of deliberate exaggeration we use when we say things such as, 'I'm dying for a cup of tea' when what we really mean is, 'I'm a bit thirsty.' It is used here in a vivid, even shocking, way. If 'looking with lust' breaks the holy law of God, you would be better off without the offending eye. If your hands are tempted to break the commandment about theft, surely you would be better off without them?

Jesus' hearers knew that he was not recommending actual physical mutilation, but making a telling point about our ethical priorities. The law of God requires more than simply observing the rules. Inner obedience, driven by love of God, is the message of this sermon.

Reflection

Temptation will be a feature of our lives as long as we live, but it is still true that where we look and what we touch is under our own control.

David Winter

99

The sin against the Holy Spirit

Then they brought to [Jesus] a demoniac who was blind and mute; and he cured him, so that the one who had been mute could speak and see. All the crowds were amazed and said, 'Can this be the Son of David?' But when the Pharisees heard it, they said, 'It is only by Beelzebul, the ruler of the demons, that this fellow casts out the demons.' He knew what they were thinking and said to them, 'Every kingdom divided against itself is laid waste... If Satan casts out Satan, he is divided against himself; how then will his kingdom stand?... But if it is by the Spirit of God that I cast out demons, then the kingdom of God has come to you... Therefore I tell you, people will be forgiven for every sin and blasphemy, but blasphemy against the Spirit will not be forgiven.'

When I was a parish priest, from time to time people would come to me convinced that they had committed the unforgivable 'sin against the Holy Spirit'. Ten minutes of studying this passage in Matthew's Gospel was usually enough to convince them that they had not done so. I hope that they went away instead with the very positive words of Jesus ringing in their ears: 'people will be forgiven for every sin and blasphemy' (v. 31) rather than the grim but specific warning from the Saviour's mouth about 'blasphemy against the Spirit' (v. 31).

Once again, the context should make the meaning of this verse plain. Jesus, by the power of the Holy Spirit, had healed a blind and mute 'demoniac'. Whatever was evil in the man had been expelled. Released from inner darkness he could now see and speak. 'All the crowds' were mightily impressed, but not some Pharisees, who asserted that the miracle had been done by invoking the power of Beelzebul, 'the ruler of the demons'. In other words, they attributed a mighty act of the Holy Spirit to a servant of Satan—a perverse, deliberate and blasphemous rejection of the truth.

Reflection

The sin here is not doubting the miracle, but saying that what was plainly good came from what was plainly evil.

DAVID WINTER

The eye of a needle

When Jesus heard this, he said to [the young man], 'There is still one thing lacking. Sell all that you own and distribute the money to the poor, and you will have treasure in heaven; then come, follow me.' But when he heard this, he became sad; for he was very rich. Jesus looked at him and said, 'How hard it is for those who have wealth to enter the kingdom of God! Indeed, it is easier for a camel to go through the eye of a needle than for someone who is rich to enter the kingdom of God.' Those who heard it said, 'Then who can be saved?' He replied, 'What is impossible for mortals is possible for God.'

A wealthy 'ruler' had asked Jesus what he must do to inherit eternal life. Jesus had directed him to the commandments, which the man said he had kept 'from his youth'. Our passage is Jesus' response to that claim. For this person, there was still 'one thing lacking' (v. 22)—his wealth. He must dispose of it, give it to the poor and simply follow Jesus. He 'became sad' (v. 23) and went away for he simply could not imagine life without those riches. They were, in the final analysis, more important to him even than eternal life. As he left, Jesus remarked to his disciples that it is 'hard' for those who are rich to enter the kingdom of God—indeed, it is as hard as squeezing a camel through the eye of a needle (another example of hyperbole!).

What is clear from the New Testament is that there is no absolute barrier to wealthy people where salvation is concerned. Wealthy women disciples supported Jesus 'out of their resources' (Luke 8:3). Those secret disciples Nicodemus and Joseph of Arimathea were wealthy. Even the tax collector Zacchaeus was accepted after giving 'half' his ill-gotten gains away (19:8). The key, it seems, is to be found in 1 Timothy 6:10: 'the love of money is a root of all kinds of evil'. The problem is not money, but the love of it.

Reflection

Money is neutral, like a skill or talent: a useful servant, a deadly master.

DAVID WINTER

A question of image

So [the scribes and chief priests] watched him and sent spies who pretended to be honest, in order to trap him by what he said, so as to hand him over to the jurisdiction and authority of the governor. So they asked him, 'Teacher, we know that you are right in what you say and teach, and you show deference to no one, but teach the way of God in accordance with truth. Is it lawful for us to pay taxes to the emperor, or not?' But he perceived their craftiness and said to them, 'Show me a denarius. Whose head and whose title does it bear?' They said, 'The emperor's.' He said to them, 'Then give to the emperor the things that are the emperor's, and to God the things that are God's.'

The fawning introduction to the question fooled no one, least of all Jesus. They wanted to trap him into making a statement that would either lose him popular support (no one likes paying taxes, especially to an occupying power) or cause him to be arrested for encouraging people to evade taxation. Asking for a coin, Jesus enquired whose image was on it. 'The emperor's', they replied, who was Caesar.

Then, said Jesus, they should give to Caesar what bears his image. After all, it came from the Roman mint. More pertinently, however, they should give to God what bears his image. The Jewish crowd knew their scriptures. Men and women are made in God's 'image'. Instead of worrying about what they owed to Caesar, Jesus was urging them to remember what they owed to God—their very existence. The whole human race comes from the divine 'mint'.

The Greek word for 'image' here is our word 'icon'. It's used of Jesus in Hebrews 1:3: he is an 'icon', a perfect image of God. To be made in the image of God is our highest calling, and to give him his due is our greatest privilege.

Reflection

It is a dereliction of our civic duty to be a tax evader. It is a dereliction of our Christian calling to forget that we bear the stamp of God's divine nature.

DAVID WINTER

A question of priorities

Now large crowds were travelling with him; and he turned and said to them, 'Whoever comes to me and does not hate father and mother, wife and children, brothers and sisters, yes, and even life itself, cannot be my disciple. Whoever does not carry the cross and follow me cannot be my disciple. For which of you, intending to build a tower, does not first sit down and estimate the cost, to see whether he has enough to complete it? Otherwise, when he has laid a foundation and is not able to finish, all who see it will begin to ridicule him, saying, "This fellow began to build and was not able to finish."'

There is, in the Gospels of Matthew, Mark and Luke, a clear change of emphasis in the narrative after the transfiguration of Jesus has taken place. Until that point, Jesus had been calling people to accept the message of the kingdom of God and had gathered together a band of disciples, men and women, who were travelling with him. Now, however, his reputation had grown so fast that he was besieged by literally thousands of people, 'so that they trampled on one other' (Luke 12:1). He still welcomed sinners and ate with them (15:2), but the crowds who treated him as a celebrity worried Jesus. He knew, and had always said, that following him involved sacrifice. It was a choice that was costly. Dark and testing times lay ahead. How could he challenge the crowds to see what it really meant to follow him?

So, once again, he turned to the use of hyperbole. Of course he did not really want people to 'hate' their parents (his last human act, as he died, was to provide, with loving care, for his mother—see John 19:26–27), but people had to count the cost of discipleship. They had to accept that following him meant walking the way of the cross, not joining in a victory procession. This commitment might well challenge even existing bonds of household, family and friendship.

Reflection

'If any want to become my followers, let them deny themselves and take up their cross and follow me' (Mark 8:34).

DAVID WINTER

The way to the Father

Thomas said to him, 'Lord, we do not know where you are going. How can we know the way?' Jesus said to him, 'I am the way, and the truth, and the life. No one comes to the Father except through me. If you know me, you will know my Father also. From now on you do know him and have seen him.' Philip said to him, 'Lord, show us the Father, and we will be satisfied.' Jesus said to him, 'Have I been with you all this time, Philip, and you still do not know me? Whoever has seen me has seen the Father.'

Well, this all seems very straightforward, especially the 'I am' saying of Jesus: 'I am the way, the truth and the life' (v. 6). Jesus is the way to God, the truth about God and the life of God.

Many years ago I was working in Jerusalem on a radio programme. A colleague asked an Arab man in the street the way to the Damascus Gate. The man simply said, 'I am the way', took his elbow and led him there. That seemed to me a wonderful exposition of the first of those sayings. Jesus does not just tell us or even show us the way to the Father. He is it: the path, the track and a companion guide.

For some people the problem comes with the next sentence: 'No one comes to the Father except through me' (v. 6). Does that mean only those who have believed in Jesus can 'come to the Father'? What about David, Moses, Abraham: are they not 'with the Father'? What about all the vast numbers of people who have never heard of Jesus or else not in any way that they could connect with? However holy their lives or fervent their prayers, will they not be able to 'come to the Father'?

I am sure it is possible (Romans 2:14–16). Richard Burridge, in his *People's Bible Commentary: John* (BRF, 2010), put it like this: 'Whenever anyone finds truth and life in God they come through the way of Jesus, whether they realise it or not'.

Reflection

There is only one Saviour and that is Jesus—one way, one truth, one life— but there are many, many ways to him.

DAVID WINTER

Pearls before swine

'Do not judge, so that you may not be judged. For with the judgement you make you will be judged, and the measure you give will be the measure you get. Why do you see the speck in your neighbour's eye, but do not notice the log in your own eye? Or how can you say to your neighbour, "Let me take the speck out of your eye", while the log is in your own eye? You hypocrite, first take the log out of your own eye, and then you will see clearly to take the speck out of your neighbour's eye. Do not give what is holy to dogs; and do not throw your pearls before swine, or they will trample them under foot and turn and maul you.'

This collection of sayings from Jesus' Sermon on the Mount is loosely linked by the theme of judgement. The Greek word covers two ideas: condemnation and the use of our critical faculties. The first can be misused and Jesus makes the point with a warning. Those who are quick to condemn others may find themselves condemned. He then adds a ludicrous verbal cartoon. A man with a log in his eye tries to correct a man with a speck in his.

We then have an enigmatic saying that does not seem to follow on. Do not give holy things to dogs or pearls to swine. Sacred and precious things are not to be treated lightly or casually. The 'holy things' may refer to the sacred temple offerings. Pearls were regarded as the most precious of all items—Jesus likened the kingdom of heaven to a pearl of great value (Matthew 13:46). So, throw them to the pigs? Ridiculous!

These two sayings seem to relate to issues about which we have to make value judgements using our God-given critical faculties. When, where and in what circumstances is it right to reveal to people the glorious and holy truths of the kingdom? Are there circumstances where our ill-judged attempts to do so may lead to blasphemy?

Reflection

God has given us the ability to make correct judgements—not in order to condemn others, but to cultivate godly wisdom.

DAVID WINTER

On the way to being saints!

'You have heard that it was said, "You shall love your neighbour and hate your enemy." But I say to you, Love your enemies and pray for those who persecute you, so that you may be children of your Father in heaven; for he makes his sun rise on the evil and on the good, and sends rain on the righteous and on the unright-eous. For if you love those who love you, what reward do you have? Do not even the tax collectors do the same? And if you greet only your brothers and sisters, what more are you doing than others? Do not even the Gentiles do the same? Be perfect, there-fore, as your heavenly Father is perfect.'

The main thrust of the Sermon on the Mount is clear enough—it sets out what citizenship of the kingdom of heaven requires. All through (but most clearly in 5:17–48), Jesus is contrasting what is expected of his disciples—the 'you' in verse 44 is emphatic in the original Greek—with the 'tax collectors' (v. 47) and 'Gentiles' (v. 47) and the Pharisees (v. 20) who simply obey the letter of the Law
. This is about a radical new ethic, which is the holiness of the kingdom. So, the whole argument ends with a 'therefore' because this is what is required and nothing less than perfection will meet the divine stand-ards. The command stands out in shocking bluntness: 'Be perfect, therefore, as your heavenly Father is perfect' (v. 48).

We cannot be perfect! The word translated as 'perfect', however, has a deeper meaning than simply 'morally faultless'. This is the only time that Matthew uses it, but Paul employs it three times—twice translated in the New Revised Standard Version as 'mature' and once as 'adults' (see 1 Corinthians 2:6; 14:20; Philippians 3:15). It speaks not of a faultless life now (something that is impossible for sinners, even redeemed ones!) but growth towards a goal. As the first epistle of John tells us, 'when he is revealed, we will be like him' (3:2)—but not yet!

Reflection

Paul greeted the Christians in Rome and Corinth as those who were 'called to be saints' (Romans 1:7; I Corinthians 1:2). That is it—we are on the way to holiness!

DAVID WINTER

The gentleness of God

What does the word 'gentleness' bring to your mind? Perhaps it would be helpful to start by saying what gentleness is *not*: it is neither weakness nor passivity, nor a lack of mental force. Gentleness can be defined as mildness and tenderness. To be gentle-hearted is to be of a kind disposition, having a humble temper that is neither sharp nor bitter. Gentleness encompasses compassion, self-control and patience.

God's inclination towards those he has made is one of immeasurable compassion and kindness, of mercy and tenderness, of unfailing love. We must remember, however, that this is only one side of the coin. God is strong in his gentleness. God is not only merciful but also just, the judge of all the earth (Genesis 18:25). In him righteousness and peace kiss (Psalm 85:10). The God of peace (Romans 15:33) is also a warrior (Exodus 15:3). He may be the potter gently shaping us (Isaiah 64:8), but he is also the refiner (Malachi 3:2–3). The God who speaks with a gentle whisper (1 Kings 19:12–13) also has a voice of thunder (Job 37:4). Our God, who will not snuff out a smouldering wick (Isaiah 42:3), is also described as a consuming fire (Deuteronomy 4:24). The Jesus who took children in his arms (Mark 10:16) also overturned the tables of the money-changers (Mark 11:15). Jesus, the Lamb of God (John 1:29, 36), is also the Lion of Judah (Revelation 5:5). The gentle breeze of the Holy Spirit (John 3:8) may also be the violent wind (Acts 2:2). We are the much-loved children of God (John 1:12), so we are disciplined as a father disciplines a child in whom he delights (Hebrew 12:5–7). We need to bear all of this in mind as we explore the gentleness of God the Father, God the Son and God the Holy Spirit.

It can be easy to develop a false image of God that we then carry, maybe subconsciously, for years. As we look at the gentleness of God, may we come to a fuller understanding of God's character. An appreciation of God's gentleness gives us confidence to approach him, ask for forgiveness and receive newness of life.

Fiona Stratta

The Father of compassion

The Lord is compassionate and gracious, slow to anger, abounding in love. He will not always accuse, nor will he harbour his anger for ever; he does not treat us as our sins deserve or repay us according to our iniquities. For as high as the heavens are above the earth, so great is his love for those who fear him; as far as the east is from the west, so far has he removed our transgressions from us. As a father has compassion on his children, so the Lord has compassion on those who fear him; for he knows how we are formed, he remembers that we are dust.

David wrote these words having experienced God's mercy. He had known what it was to displease God and have experienced for himself God's forgiveness and continued blessing. He was familiar with God's compassion, finding in his relationship with God the tenderness of a father. His understanding of God's character was in accord with how God revealed himself to Moses, as 'the Lord, the compassionate and gracious God, slow to anger, abounding in love and faithfulness, maintaining love to thousands, and forgiving wickedness, rebellion and sin. Yet he does not leave the guilty unpunished' (Exodus 34:6–7).

God had many names in the Old Testament. It is David who recognises in God a father who understands the frailty of his children and deals with them gently. Perhaps we take the concept of God as our heavenly Father for granted, for we have the perspective of the New Testament available to us. For instance, we know that Jesus instructed his disciples to start their prayers with the words, 'Our Father in heaven' (Matthew 6:9). We also know that we can cry out to God using the intimate name 'Abba, Father' (Romans 8:15) and we understand that, by receiving and believing in Christ, we become the children of God (John 1:12).

Prayer

'Praise be to the God and Father of our Lord Jesus Christ, the Father of compassion and the God of all comfort, who comforts us in all our troubles, so that we can comfort those in any trouble with the comfort we ourselves have received from God' (2 Corinthians 1:3–4). Amen

FIONA STRATTA

The nurturing heart of God

'Can a mother forget the baby at her breast and have no compassion on the child she has borne? Though she may forget, I will not forget you! See, I have engraved you on the palms of my hands... As a mother comforts her child, so will I comfort you; and you will be comforted over Jerusalem.'

Although the Bible contains mainly male metaphors for God, there are a few maternal figures of speech to be found, too. In these verses, God expresses his tender love for his people through the image of a mother's love for her child—a selfless, unconditional, devoted, gentle, comforting and nurturing love. The mother gives herself to her child, providing care and protection, a place of safety and rest. Even if human love as great as this breaks down, God's love for us is unwavering.

Our response to such love is to still ourselves before him, regularly seeking solitude and silence. By this means, we can remain in a spiritual place where we can receive from and be nurtured by God.

The image of a mother and child is developed further in Psalm 131 (v. 2), where David expresses the trust and contentment that he has found in resting in God: 'But I have stilled and quietened my soul; like a weaned child with its mother, like a weaned child is my soul within me.'

'The Lord is good to all, he has compassion on all he has made' (Psalm 145:9). We read in Matthew 6:26 and 28 that even the birds and flowers are gently nurtured by God. In view of this, Jesus urges us not to be anxious about our daily requirements, for our heavenly Father knows what we need. This sets us free to focus on 'his kingdom and his righteousness' (v. 33): we are free to live, laugh, give, love and serve him. We start to experience what it is like to receive the kingdom of heaven like a little child, trusting and secure (Mark 10:15).

Reflection

Father-like, he tends and spares us; well our feeble frame he knows,
in his hands he gently bears us, rescues us from all our foes.

Henry Francis Lyte, 1834
FIONA STRATTA

El Shaddai

> When Abram was ninety-nine years old, the Lord appeared to him and said, 'I am God Almighty; walk before me faithfully and be blameless. Then I will make my covenant between me and you and will greatly increase your numbers.'... And God said to [Jacob], 'I am God Almighty; be fruitful and increase in number. A nation and a community of nations will come from you, and kings will be among your descendants.'... [Jacob said] 'Because of the Almighty, who blesses you with blessings of the skies above, blessings of the deep springs below, blessings of the breast and womb.'

In each case above, the Hebrew translated as 'God Almighty' is 'El Shaddai'. 'El' is the Hebrew word for God and the word 'Shaddai' tells of a particular attribute of God. There has been much discussion about the precise meaning of 'El Shaddai'. The word 'shad' means all-powerful and invincible, but 'shad' also means 'breast', the place of sustenance and comfort, of fruitfulness and blessing. Hence, 'El Shaddai' reveals both the power of God and the blessing of God. The blessings of El Shaddai were passed down through the generations... to Abraham, Isaac, Jacob, Joseph and beyond.

Interestingly, the title El Shaddai appears more often in the book of Job than in any other. As Job learned of God's awe-inspiring power, he also experienced God's faithfulness and restoration. Likewise, God draws near to comfort us in our anguish, to restore and bless us.

The 17th-century lay Carmelite Brother Lawrence enjoyed such an intimate relationship with God as he 'practised the presence of God' that he knew inexpressible happiness. Such was the serenity of the experience that he likened it to a babe at his mother's breast. We, too, can drink and feed on Christ, the living water, the bread of life. We can 'Taste and see that the Lord is good' (Psalm 34:8) and know comfort, sustenance, fruitfulness and blessing.

Reflection

'The Lord bless you and keep you; the Lord make his face shine on you and be gracious to you; the Lord turn his face towards you and give you peace'
(Numbers 6:24–26).

FIONA STRATTA

Under his wings and on his wings

In a desert land he found him, in a barren and howling waste. He shielded him and cared for him; he guarded him as the apple of his eye, like an eagle that stirs up its nest and hovers over its young, that spreads its wings to catch them and carries them on its pinions... He will cover you with his feathers, and under his wings you will find refuge; his faithfulness will be your shield and rampart.

The gentleness of God is also seen in the image we find used in scripture of a bird caring for its young, providing them with shelter and protection from harm. Safe under the parental wings, the baby birds are comforted by the softness of the feathers. Having said that, the gentle image is immediately followed by an image of war. When we are in the thick of it, God will be our strength, our shield, our rampart.

The image of the eagle stirring up the nest in order to get its young to fly reminds us that God nudges us from our 'nests', out of our comfort zones, so that we can soar towards his purposes for us. As the mother eagle will hover below her young, ready to scoop up on her wings any that are falling, taking them back to the heights where she will encourage them to fly again, so God 'catches' and 'lifts' us. Our response is to trust and take refuge in God's faithfulness, to take action when prompted, knowing that underneath are the everlasting arms.

Jesus also used the image of a bird, this time a hen, as he was grieving over Jerusalem and their rejection of God. We see in his words his desire to gently comfort and provide for all his people: 'How often have I desired to gather your children together as a hen gathers her brood under her wings, and you were not willing!' (Matthew 23:37).

Reflection

Praise to the Lord, who doth nourish thy life and restore thee,
fitting thee well for the tasks that are ever before thee.
Then to thy need,
God as a mother doth speed,
spreading the wings of grace o'er thee.

Joachim Neander, 1680

FIONA STRATTA

111

God: our provider and peace

> Abraham looked up and there in a thicket he saw a ram caught by its horns. He went over and took the ram and sacrificed it as a burnt offering instead of his son. So Abraham called that place The Lord Will Provide... But the Lord said to [Gideon], 'Peace! Do not be afraid. You are not going to die.' So Gideon built an altar to the Lord there and called it The Lord Is Peace.

In our first passage, God is named as Yahweh-Yireh. The word 'Yireh', 'provider', incorporates the meanings of the Latin *pro* and *video*, 'to see before'. God sees what will be needed before a situation even arises and then gently provides. We may have to wait until the last moment for God's intervention, as Abraham did, but, whatever the circumstances, we can hold on to the promise that God has already seen and will meet our needs, 'according to his glorious riches in Christ Jesus' (Philippians 4:19).

In our second passage, 'The Lord is Peace' is from the Hebrew 'Yahweh-Shalom'. 'Shalom' can be translated as 'completeness' as well as 'peace', giving us a picture of wholeness, blessing, safety, rest and well-being. Peace is so much more than the absence of conflict. We all long for 'shalom' and God, in his love and gentleness, 'delights in the well-being of his servant' (Psalm 35:27) by blessing us with peace.

In Colossians 3:15–17, we are given guidance on how the peace of Christ can reign in our hearts: by being thankful and singing to God with gratitude, by allowing God's words to penetrate deeply into our hearts and by doing everything in the name of the Lord Jesus. We are 'called to peace' (v. 15); God's longing is that we know shalom and trust in his provision. These go hand-in-hand, for if we can trust God for all our needs in our journey through life, we will experience shalom.

Prayer

Lord, in your gentleness you assure us of your provision and offer us peace. In you we have a hiding-place, a shelter from the storms of life. May your words reach not only our heads but also our hearts. May we experience the well-being that you desire for us. Amen

FIONA STRATTA

The gentleness of the shepherd

The Lord is my shepherd, I lack nothing. He makes me lie down in green pastures, he leads me beside quiet waters, he refreshes my soul. He guides me along the right paths for his name's sake. Even though I walk through the darkest valley, I will fear no evil, for you are with me; your rod and your staff, they comfort me. You prepare a table before me in the presence of my enemies. You anoint my head with oil; my cup overflows. Surely your goodness and love will follow me all the days of my life, and I will dwell in the house of the Lord for ever.

The metaphor of God as a shepherd, and we as his sheep, is found throughout the Bible, with perhaps the best-loved passage being Psalm 23, which our passage for today comes from.

The shepherd provides for the needs of the flock, finding places for his sheep to rest and drink, taking them under the shade of trees in the heat of the day.

In the same way, God restores us with a gentle touch. The shepherds from that time and part of the world traditionally led their flocks from the front rather than driving them from behind. If we watch and listen here, God leads us in the same way—he does not drive us or force us to follow in his ways. The dark valleys that we inevitably go through lead on to new green pastures. We are defended with the rod and guided by the staff.

The erring sheep is carried back to the flock on the shepherd's shoulders (Luke 15:3–7). He has special tenderness for those who cannot defend themselves—the young and those caring for the young: 'He tends his flock like a shepherd: He gathers the lambs in his arms and carries them close to his heart; he gently leads those that have young' (Isaiah 40:11). Our shepherd is strong, yet he is also tender.

Reflection

Reflect on these words from Psalm 54:4: 'Surely God is my help; the Lord is the one who sustains me.' Thank the Lord for times in our lives when we have had a sense of being gently sustained and 'carried' by him.

FIONA STRATTA

113

Jesus: the good shepherd

When [Jesus] saw the crowds, he had compassion on them, because they were harassed and helpless, like sheep without a shepherd… 'I am the good shepherd. The good shepherd lays down his life for the sheep… I am the good shepherd; I know my sheep and my sheep know me—just as the Father knows me and I know the Father—and I lay down my life for the sheep.'

In the first verse of the passage here, we see God the Son full of compassion for the stressed, the needy and those lacking direction. Once again, we come across the image of the shepherd, so familiar to Jesus' listeners from their daily lives. Jesus has already described himself as the gate for the sheep (John 10:7). The shepherd, in placing himself in the entrance to the sheepfold, blocked its access and was ready to protect the sheep from attack, risking his life for them. Now we learn that, such is Jesus' commitment to his sheep, he is willing to die for them. He will lay down his life gently, without struggle or retaliation, without words of self-defence; he will go quietly, like a lamb being led to the slaughter, like a sheep silent before its shearers (Isaiah 53:7).

The God of justice, who cannot clear the guilty by simply overlooking wrongdoing, in his love and mercy set up a sacrificial system by which he could forgive sin. This foreshadowed the sacrifice of the Lamb of God on the cross, the most powerful declaration of both God's justice and his mercy, making God's grace available to all.

We have but to respond by finding salvation by entering the 'gate', going in and out and finding pasture (John 10:9). Then we can live in the way God desires, which is, 'To act justly and to love mercy and to walk humbly with your God' (Micah 6:8).

Prayer

'May the God of peace, who, by the blood of the eternal covenant brought back from the dead our Lord Jesus, that great Shepherd of the sheep, equip you with everything good for doing his will and may he work in us what is pleasing to him… Amen' (Hebrews 13:20–21).

FIONA STRATTA

Jesus: gentle and humble

[Jesus said] 'Come to me, all you who are weary and burdened, and I will give you rest. Take my yoke upon me and learn from me, for I am gentle and humble in heart, and you will find rest for your souls. For my yoke is easy and my burden is light.'... [Jesus] said to them, 'Come with me by yourselves to a quiet place and get some rest.'

In looking at Jesus' words and actions, we discover more of what God is like, for scripture tells us that 'the Son is the radiance of God's glory and the exact representation of his being' (Hebrews 1:3).

In the above verses, Jesus uses two adjectives to describe himself: 'gentle' and 'humble' (Matthew 11:29). Perhaps we are surprised by his choice of words—after all, there are so many others he could have used—yet these are the qualities that he wishes us to recognise in him.

The company of gentle and humble people is restful: we can relax, lay down our burdens and any pretence. Similarly, Jesus promises us that, in coming to him, we will find rest for our souls and, by spending time with him in a quiet place, we will be restored. Any work of restoration has to be carried out gently.

Instead of experiencing freedom in Christ, however, we have a tendency to be burdened by a 'yoke of slavery' (Galatians 5:1). That is, we carry our own heavy burdens, allowing ourselves to be weighed down by thoughts and anxieties or false ideas about God and Christian living. It is a paradox to think of being yoked as being restful and giving freedom, but, in being yoked with Christ, we do not pull alone. Instead, we find strength, peace and rest in his help and in the rhythm of moving alongside him at his pace, learning from him and casting our cares on him (Psalm 55:22), recognising him as a friend and companion.

Reflection

'Now the Lord is the Spirit, and where the Spirit of the Lord is, there is freedom. And we, who with unveiled faces all reflect the Lord's glory, are being transformed into his likeness' (2 Corinthians 3:17–18).

FIONA STRATTA

Jesus: the tender shoot

A shoot will come up from the stump of Jesse; from his roots a Branch will bear fruit. The Spirit of the Lord will rest on him—the Spirit of wisdom and understanding, the Spirit of counsel and of might, the Spirit of the knowledge and fear of the Lord—and he will delight in the fear of the Lord... The wolf will live with the lamb, the leopard will lie down with the goat, the calf and the lion and the yearling together; and a little child will lead them... He grew up before him like a tender shoot, and like a root out of dry ground.

These words, speaking of the coming Messiah, point to the tender, gentle ways that will characterise him. Full of the Spirit, he will speak powerfully and wisely, showing us how to live in a way that will honour God. Familiar with suffering, he will carry our sorrows, heal us through his own wounds and be crushed for our wrongdoing. The tender shoot will be uprooted for our sakes, but, as a result, many will find peace with God (Isaiah 53:3–7). Jesus chose to become vulnerable here; in his strength, he was gentle.

God longs to take the hardness of our hearts and give us tender hearts, like the heart of his own Son. He promised, through the prophet Ezekiel (36:26–27), 'I will give you a new heart and put a new spirit in you; I will remove from you your heart of stone and give you a heart of flesh. And I will put my Spirit in you.' Through his Spirit, we are transformed into those who are characterised by forgiveness and compassion.

Jesus, the tender shoot, shows us the way of gentleness. He likens the growth of the kingdom of God in us to a mustard seed—a tiny seed that grows so large it can shelter many birds. Jesus' gentle ways draw us to him and stir us to follow him. As we grow in his likeness, discovering more of his love, so we become those who can offer shelter and protection to others.

Prayer

Lord, soften our hearts; through your Spirit give us hearts of flesh. Amen

FIONA STRATTA

Gentle as the dove

Then John gave this testimony: 'I saw the Spirit come down from
heaven as a dove and remain on him. And I myself did not know
him, but the one who sent me to baptise with water told me, "The
man on whom you see the Spirit come down and remain is the
one who will baptise with the Holy Spirit." I have seen and I testify
that this is God's Chosen One.'

We now turn to look at the gentleness of God as seen in the Holy Spirit,
who came down to Jesus in the form of what is traditionally considered
the gentlest of birds, the dove. It has become a symbol of peace and is
regarded as an affectionate bird, innocent of any vicious ways (Matthew
10:16).

In Luke's account of the baptism of Jesus, we read that God spoke
words of love and affirmation over his Son—'You are my Son, whom I
love; with you I am well pleased' (3:22)—and Jesus was filled with the
Holy Spirit (4:1), ready to overcome temptation and start his ministry.

Jesus told us of the coming of the Holy Spirit to indwell in all who
are his. He refers to the Holy Spirit as the Paraclete, which is translated
as 'the Helper', 'the Advocate', 'the Comforter' and 'the Counsellor',
who comes alongside and gently helps and encourages us in our daily
lives (John 14:16; 16:7). The Holy Spirit points us to Jesus and reminds
us of his words.

As we live by the Spirit, the fruits of the Holy Spirit grow within us.
Gentleness is one of the fruits of the spirit, alongside love, joy, peace,
patience, kindness, goodness, faithfulness and self-control (Galatians
5:22). We are urged to be gentle in all our dealings with people—'Let
your gentleness be evident to all' (Philippians 4:5)—and taught that
there is great power in a gentle answer, for it 'turns away wrath'
(Proverbs 15:1).

Prayer

*Lord, in your gentleness, you have promised that you are 'close to the
broken-hearted and save those who are crushed in spirit' (Psalm 34:18).
We thank you for the helper who gently comes alongside us. Grow in us
that same gentleness. Amen*

FIONA STRATTA

117

Long-suffering God

When God saw what they did and how they turned from their evil ways, he relented and did not bring on them the destruction he had threatened. But to Jonah this seemed very wrong, and he became angry. He prayed to the Lord, 'Isn't this what I said, Lord, when I was still at home? That is what I tried to forestall by fleeing to Tarshish. I knew that you are a gracious and compassionate God, slow to anger and abounding in love, a God who relents from sending calamity.'

Throughout the Bible narrative we see evidence of the gentleness of God in his long-suffering ways. In these verses, Jonah speaks of God being 'slow to anger' (4:2), ready to relent from punishing those who turn to him. We read in 2 Peter 3:9 that, 'The Lord… is patient… not wanting anyone to perish, but everyone to come to repentance.' Moses, David and the prophets Jeremiah, Joel and Nahum all recognised that, although God cannot leave the guilty unpunished, his dealings with humanity are characterised by a long-suffering approach. God is indeed gracious, compassionate and abounding in love.

Jonah resents the magnitude of God's mercy, describing it as being available even to the inhabitants of Nineveh in Assyria, the enemies of his people and well known for their wickedness. Initially he tried to run from God's assignment (to tell those in Nineveh that God saw their atrocities and would take action unless they repented of their evil ways). God, however, is 'slow to anger' and gives Jonah a second chance, showing him the grace that Jonah later struggles to show to the city of Nineveh.

We see in this narrative God's long-suffering nature demonstrated to both an individual and a nation. In his faithfulness and gentleness, the God who gave Jonah a second chance will do the same for us. The fruit of the Spirit that is 'patience' (Galatians 5:22) is rendered as 'long-suffering' in the King James Version. Being long-suffering is a quality that God will chisel into our characters via our life circumstances, if we are responsive to the work of the Holy Spirit within us.

Prayer

Lord, thank you for your gentle long-suffering nature.
Make us more like you. Amen

FIONA STRATTA

LUKE 15:20–23 (NIV)

The forgiving father

So [the son] got up and went to his father. But while he was still a long way off, his father saw him and was filled with compassion for him; he ran to his son, threw his arms around him and kissed him. The son said to him, 'Father, I have sinned against heaven and against you. I am no longer worthy to be called your son.' But the father said to his servants, 'Quick! Bring the best robe and put it on him. Put a ring on his finger and sandals on his feet. Bring the fattened calf and kill it. Let's have a feast and celebrate.'

The father in Jesus' story demonstrates several characteristics that are linked closely to gentleness. He is compassionate and has a long-suffering nature; his response to his errant son is tender, loving and forgiving, full of grace and mercy. We also see the father's joy as he eagerly welcomes and provides for his son, arranging a lavish celebration. In these few verses, Jesus paints a picture of our heavenly Father—someone who is not solemn or severe, but full of gentleness and joy.

The story goes on to relate how the father's reaction to his elder son's resentment is correspondingly gentle: 'You are always with me, and everything I have is yours' (v. 31). It is a puzzle to him that his firstborn cannot understand his joy, his generosity and his grace. After all, the elder son has not lived one day without knowing the open-handed love of his father.

We do not know how the elder son responded; but what is our own response to our heavenly Father? We can rest assured of his gentle welcome and delight in us when we return to him, aware of our failings. Even during the times when we feel bitter or resentful, missing the daily signs of God's goodness in our lives, he gently asks us to join in the feast, wanting us to be a part of the celebration.

Prayer

Lord, your word tells us that you prepare a table for us, inviting us to taste and see you are good. Enable us to respond to your gentle invitation. Amen
(See Psalm 23:5; 34:8.)

FIONA STRATTA

Gentleness in word and action

When he arrived at the house of Jairus, he did not let anyone go in with him except Peter, John and James, and the child's father and mother. Meanwhile, all the people were wailing and mourning for her. 'Stop wailing,' Jesus said. 'She is not dead but asleep.' They laughed at him, knowing that she was dead. But he took her by the hand and said, 'My child, get up!' Her spirit returned, and at once she stood up. Then Jesus told them to give her something to eat.

In both his teaching and actions, Jesus revealed the unlimited, tender love of God. We see gentleness in his actions and reactions to people (unless he was aware of hypocrisy, which he spoke out against in no uncertain terms). Jesus' acts regarding the vulnerable stemmed from compassion. He showed gentleness to the widow whose son had died, the women bringing their children to him, the blind and the deaf. Similarly, at the raising of Jairus' daughter, we see Jesus sensitively considering the needs of the parents, taking them and only three disciples into the room, and we see his gentleness with the girl as he takes her hand, gives her life and instructs her parents to give her some food.

It is possible that, in our care and concern, we can rush into situations with insufficient sensitivity. We need to develop gentleness in both our speech and actions. It is written in 1 Peter 3:15, 'Always be prepared to give an answer to everyone who asks you to give a reason for the hope that you have. But do this with gentleness and respect.' Not only do we wear the 'full armour of God' (the belt of truth, the breastplate of righteousness, the shield of faith, the helmet of salvation and the sword of the Sprit, described in Ephesians 6:11–17) but we are also to 'clothe' ourselves with 'compassion, kindness, humility, gentleness and patience' (Colossians 3:12). Without these 'clothes' our words and actions may become harsh.

Prayer

Lord, warm our hearts with your love and energise us to carry out all our activities 'clothed' in godly virtues. May our actions be sensitive, stemming from your tender compassion. Amen

FIONA STRATTA

Love is at the heart of gentleness

Love is patient, love is kind. It does not envy, it does not boast, it is not proud. It does not dishonour others, it is not self-seeking, it is not easily angered, it keeps no record of wrongs. Love does not delight in evil but rejoices with the truth. It always protects, always trusts, always hopes, always perseveres. Love never fails... God is love. Whoever lives in love lives in God, and God in them... We love because he first loved us.

Scripture tells us that God is love and, in this well-known and definitive description of love, we see the characteristics that we have been exploring as we have looked at the gentleness of God: patience, kindness, humility, protection, provision, mercy and faithfulness. Love is at the heart of gentleness: love is gentle; to be gentle is to be loving.

Our perception of God will affect how we respond to God, ourselves and others. If we see God as punitive, judgemental or severe, then we will not only cower before him but also our attitudes to ourselves and others will reflect the harsh picture we hold of God. We are likely to be hard-hearted and judgemental.

As his dearly loved children, God desires us to respond to him from love, not from fear, for 'perfect love drives out fear' (1 John 4:18). Children tend to imitate their parents in their behaviour. If we perceive our Father God's love and gentleness towards us, we will 'Be imitators of God... and live a life of love, just as Christ loved us' (Ephesians 5:1). By the Holy Spirit's work within us, we will love God, and treat ourselves and others gently. We will be able to fulfil the two greatest commandments: 'Love the Lord your God with all your heart and with all your soul and with all your mind' and 'Love your neighbour as yourself' (Matthew 22:37–39).

Reflection

Reflect on Paul's words, which remind us of the supremacy of love: 'over all these virtues put on love, which binds them all together in perfect unity' (Colossians 3:14); 'And now these three remain: faith, hope and love. But the greatest of these is love' (1 Corinthians 13:13).

FIONA STRATTA

Mystery and secrecy in Mark

Going to university was a tremendous adventure for me; it was then that I began maturing as a human being and realising that the Christian faith was much bigger and more exciting than I had hitherto believed. Then came my encounter with theology—the subject that I had opted to study for three years. What an eye-opener that was! Church life had largely focused on worship and youth activities. Now came the chance to wrestle with so much that was new. The course I had embarked on centred on the traditional menu of theological topics—Bible, doctrine, history, languages and philosophy—and equipped me to devote much of my subsequent life to exploring theology in all its richness and diversity.

My original expectation was that it would be pretty straightforward. After all, the Bible was simple, wasn't it? A collection of books that told a particular story? I could not have been further from the truth! From the outset I found it exhilarating and the avenue along which I found myself travelling mostly was that of the New Testament. The unfolding of Jesus' life and ministry was not as simple as I had originally thought. There was conflict, there were potential contradictions, there was mis-understanding, even among the twelve disciples. Then there was also a secret that could not yet be shared openly.

It is that 'secret' that I want to explore in the following pages—the 'messianic secret'—as it dominated many of the conversations between Jesus and his disciples in Mark's Gospel. It fascinated me as I first encountered theology: why was it necessary to keep some information from the crowds and what could possibly be achieved by doing so? This is not an easy question to tackle, but, essentially, the idea that some-thing was being kept 'secret' arises from the several instances in which Jesus commands people to be silent about his action and identity. The whole thrust of Mark's Gospel shows that the real meaning of Jesus' messiahship became clear only with his death and resurrection. His ministry, as it developed, could not be grasped sensibly without rooting it in what had not yet taken place. To put it another way, Christmas makes no sense without Easter.

Andrew Jones

Good news

> Now after John was arrested, Jesus came to Galilee, proclaiming the good news of God, and saying, 'The time is fulfilled, and the kingdom of God has come near; repent, and believe in the good news.'

From the outset of my encounter with theology it became clear that reading the scriptures in isolation—that is, not relating the stories, experiences and themes to each other—is unhelpful. Making sense of the idea that some aspects of Jesus' identity need to be kept secret for 'the time being' is connected to understanding his proclamation that physical time and even world history was somehow at a crossroads in his ministry. This is essentially what he is saying here at the start of Mark's Gospel.

For many people this would have been seen as anything but 'good news'. For them, life was fine as it was, but for others the announce-ment was liberating. In many ways, however, such liberation needs to be shared carefully—not unleashed like a bull in a china shop!

The opening scenes of Mark's Gospel use settings and symbols with care. Mark is keen to convey that an 'invasion' of God's Spirit took place at Jesus' baptism (vv. 9–11), one that sets a new apocalyptic timescale in motion, which Jesus announces as being the moment of God's inter-vention that the people had been waiting for. This did not happen in the temple or on the steps of the royal palace or at the seat of govern-ment, however—it happened elsewhere, at the periphery.

Thus Mark generates a real sense of momentousness and also announces a new beginning and this dynamic continues right through his Gospel. Having said that, the mystery—possibly part of the secret—is that, no sooner is the fulfilment of God's kingdom announced, but the expectations thus generated are postponed or at least kept back. Although the crowd is told that 'The time is fulfilled' and the kingdom 'has come near' (v. 15), they still have to wait patiently to find out more.

Reflection

Jesus proclaims the coming of a new order, one marked by mutual respect and where differences between people are removed. Relationships are marked by equality and domination by a single group is swept away.

ANDREW JONES

A new kind of authority

> They went to Capernaum; and when the sabbath came, [Jesus]
> entered the synagogue and taught. They were astounded at his
> teaching, for he taught them as one having authority, and not as
> the scribes.

Mark describes the beginning of Jesus' public ministry in the area surrounding Galilee. Jesus summons—rather than invites—his first disciples; he reveals himself as a teacher and healer and he enters into debate
with a variety of opponents. Initially things seem to be proceeding well.
Jesus appears to be in control of the situation: he has 'authority' (v. 22).
Before long, however, his opponents will be plotting to destroy him (3:6).

Capernaum was a significant commercial centre on the border—a
cosmopolitan place where you would encounter different people, customs and values. At the centre was the synagogue, where, on the sabbath, the service would feature prayers, scripture readings and teaching.
Anyone of sufficient learning could be invited to participate. After Jesus
had spoken there, the people contrasted him favourably with the scribes,
who were interpreters and teachers of the Old Testament Law and not
simply secretaries. Jesus' teaching was more direct and more confidently
rooted in his own authority; he spoke from the heart. Intriguingly, however, from the moment he sets foot in the synagogue, it becomes clear
that his 'kingdom project' is at odds with the social order of the day.

In these opening sections of the Gospel, Mark is anxious that his
readers understand the true nature of Jesus' mission, which is to proclaim the coming of something completely new, a new way of seeing
things and relating to others, even a new way of understanding God's
relationship with the world. Mark also conveys the disciples' anxiety
about Jesus and how they constantly try and fail to 'tie him down'.
Again and again Jesus has to reaffirm his primary vocation—to proclaim
the good news in the synagogues and bring liberation to the oppressed—
but the disciples are slow to grasp the vision.

Reflection

*May we never cease to be astounded by Jesus' world order and never tire of
wanting to be part of his vision for a better world.*

ANDREW JONES

Jesus becomes known

They were all amazed, and they kept asking one another, 'What is this? A new teaching—with authority! He commands even the unclean spirits, and they obey him.' At once [Jesus'] fame began to spread throughout the surrounding region of Galilee.

As if open criticism of the social order was not enough, Jesus now proceeds to break the Law, as a way of dramatising his opposition to the scribes, the social elite and those in power. His healing of the possessed man on the sabbath (v. 25) is significant, for it involves an 'unclean' spirit that gives voice to the opposition to Jesus ('Have you come to destroy us?', v. 24) and thus paves the way for Jesus to commence his ministry of healing.

The amazement of the crowd is a hallmark of most of the healing miracles in the Gospels. The expectation at that time was for any kind of healing to involve ritual and magical displays, but not so with Jesus. He healed by word alone, thus highlighting the truly supernatural character of his miracles.

It seems that wherever Jesus was, so much was new—a new order where all were invited to participate fully; a new freedom in which all, regardless of status, could find liberation; a new teaching via which all could become disciples. Change is not an easy experience and replacing a whole social order is well-nigh impossible, but that was Jesus' mission. Given that this was the case, and no matter how much he resisted it, people wanted to know more about him.

Mark's reference to Jesus' fame spreading throughout Galilee introduces a recurring theme in the Gospel: it is this increasing fame that seems to grate for Jesus and he often resists it or tries to get away from the crowds. Again, this must have added to his disciples' frustration and caused much of their misunderstanding.

Reflection

The disciples must have been asking, 'Why hide this new power? Why not shout it from the rooftops so that everyone can benefit?' But the new order needed a firm foundation—there was much more to come. We know that because we know the end of the story; the disciples did not.

ANDREW JONES

Telling the story

> Again [Jesus] began to teach beside the lake. Such a very large crowd gathered around him that he got into a boat on the lake and sat there, while the whole crowd was beside the lake on the land. He began to teach them many things in parables.

I often think of the first three chapters of Mark's Gospel as Jesus' first 'kingdom campaign'—one that ended in polarisation and a possible family argument (3:31–35). It seems that his family was concerned about his well-being and the deteriorating situation around him. Jesus' response was that he now had a new family—those supporting him in seeking to establish the new social order. Then, once again, he retreated to the lakeside to reflect on his mission, but, as before (1:33; 2:2), the crowd followed him.

Jesus' second 'kingdom campaign' is marked by an extended sermon (4:1–34), which draws heavily on images of the land and the well-established wisdom of the farming community. It offers the gathered crowd hope in the face of mounting opposition to Jesus' 'good news' by the authorities.

In the opening part of this sermon, Jesus sits in a boat, using parables to teach the crowd gathered on the shore. Mark tells us that this is how Jesus taught his disciples in private (4:10, 34; 7:17; 9:28; 10:10; 13:3). A famous New Testament scholar, C.H. Dodd, defined 'parable' as 'a metaphor or simile drawn from nature or common life, arresting the hearer by its vividness or strangeness, and leaving the mind in sufficient doubt about its precise application to tease it into active thought'. This brings us back to the themes of secrecy, misunderstanding, privacy and seeking to make sense of all that is going on, which are so characteristic of this Gospel.

Prayer

Lord, give us strength to be your disciples today as you did to those who first followed you. Give us grace to listen to your voice and, in it, see the truth about the depth of your presence in our lives, even when you challenge us in new and baffling ways.

ANDREW JONES

Can you truly hear?

In his teaching [Jesus] said to them: 'Listen! A sower went to sow...' And he said, 'Let anyone with ears to hear listen!'

The sermon in chapter 4 introduces two themes that are central in Mark's Gospel: the commands to 'listen' and 'watch'. As that strategy unfolds, both commands come to represent the disciples' struggles to understand and follow Jesus (7:18; 8:15–21; 9:7). It is the command to 'listen' that dominates this first extended sermon, while that to 'watch' dominates the second (13:1–37).

At the heart of the first sermon lies the well-known story about sowing seeds. Jesus may have been reflecting on a passage from his own scriptures (our Old Testament), which may even have been the reading used at the Capernaum synagogue some days earlier. In that passage (Isaiah 55:10–11), Isaiah asserts that God's word goes out and does not return empty; it yields and shares. The command to 'listen' frames the parable of the sower and this again has echoes of much older scriptural traditions. In Deuteronomy 6:4, for example, God calls his people to 'hear' (a passage quoted by Mark in 12:29).

Later on, the notion of 'mystery' is introduced (4:11): the hidden meaning of the parable is only given to those who truly seek understanding. The explanation Jesus offers places the sower as the proclaimer of the kingdom, while the hostile soil represents three obstacles to the acceptance of his call to discipleship. Interestingly, though, the main focus of this parable is on the seeds and what happens to them in the different kinds of soil; the sower does not appear to be the centre of attention.

Jesus' teaching illustrates God's lavish offer of the kingdom and the mixed responses to this offer. Even so, the results are amazingly rich. He may well have used the parable as an explanation for the mixed responses to his preaching as well as a source of encouragement in the face of opposition.

Reflection

Despite everything, God's kingdom will come with marvellous abundance and the seeds planted in the good soil anticipate its coming.

ANDREW JONES

Can you truly understand?

When [Jesus] was alone, those who were around him along with the twelve asked him about the parables. And he said to them, 'To you has been given the secret of the kingdom of God, but for those outside, everything comes in parables; in order that "they may indeed look, but not perceive, and may indeed listen, but not understand; so that they may not turn again and be forgiven".' And he said to them, 'Do you not understand this parable? Then how will you understand all the parables?'

Jesus' response to those questioning him about the parable is extremely interesting and suggests a division in the audience, that some know the secret and some do not. In some ways, parables hide the secret further, blinding the listeners, preventing understanding and revealing nothing! To make matters more complex, Jesus quotes from Isaiah 6:9–10, where Isaiah responds positively to God's call, only to be told to go and tell the people to listen but not understand, to see but not perceive. Surely, however, this does not mean that God directly wills the people's stubbornness, but, rather, God has foreseen such stubbornness and incorporated it into his plan, so it should not dismay Isaiah.

Jesus has a two-fold audience. While those in the crowd understand nothing of 'the secret of the kingdom of God', this secret has been given to the disciples and they receive the necessary explanations for all the parables. The text does not suggest it is the preached word which produces this two-fold division, nor that it results from the hearers' reactions to Jesus' preaching. It is simply the case that, to the disciples, the key for understanding has been given; to the others, it has not. This may seem to contradict the overall gospel picture of the absolute inclusivity of Jesus' activity in general; the way in which he seeks fellowship with those regarded as sinners fits badly with the 'hidden meaning' aspect of parables. The question I am left with is possibly the same question with which the disciples wrestled: if the aim of the parables was to hide the core of the message, why use them at all?

Reflection

Christianity is about encountering mystery, not problem-solving.

ANDREW JONES

Can you truly see?

[Jesus] said to them, 'Is a lamp brought in to be put under the bushel basket, or under the bed, and not on the lampstand? For there is nothing hidden, except to be disclosed; nor is anything secret, except to come to light. Let anyone with ears to hear listen!'

The overall emphasis of the parable of the sower was on the barriers to discipleship, because the heart of Jesus' sermon focuses on why some people continue to reject his ministry. Was it not the case then—and still is the case today—that we all hear and interpret the gospel in our own particular contexts and respond accordingly?

However much we try to avoid acknowledging that social and economic circumstances and cultural situations influence how we hear God and respond to his call, they remain factors. History offers many examples of how men and women in their own very different contexts responded to God. On the one hand there is the example of Francis of Assisi, giving up wealth in order to become a true disciple. On the other hand, there are others who refuse to hear at all, so as to remain comfortable. We need to recognise that when we hear God's call, we are inevitably changed and nothing can be quite the same again. If we 'listen but do not hear', it is probably not because of the obscurity of the word, but because of our loyalty to our existing social context.

So it is that Mark here offers the parable of the lampstand. Following on from the parable of the sower, it balances and clarifies the interpretation of the parable of the sower. Mark is keen to assert that the term 'mystery' does not mean that the parables enshrine secret knowledge. They should not be misconstrued as a 'lamp' being hidden, but as teaching meant to illuminate and reveal (v. 22). It is precisely because this part of Jesus' sermon unveils the true loyalties of the hearer that it is polarising and, with the words 'Let anyone with ears to hear listen', the first half draws to a close.

Reflection
*How clearly do we hear God's call? How do we listen
and how do we respond?*

ANDREW JONES

The wind and sea confuse the disciples

When evening had come, [Jesus] said to them, 'Let us go across to the other side.' And leaving the crowd behind, they took him with them in the boat... A great gale arose, and the waves beat into the boat... But he was in the stern, asleep on the cushion; and they woke him up and said, 'Teacher, do you not care that we are perishing?' He woke up and rebuked the wind, and said to the sea, 'Peace! Be still!' Then the wind ceased, and there was a dead calm. He said to them, 'Why are you afraid? Have you still no faith?' And they were filled with great awe and said to one another, 'Who then is this, that even the wind and sea obey him?'

This is one of six boat trips in Mark's Gospel, although only two contain detail—this one and the one to Bethsaida (6:45–53). Interestingly, in both these trips Mark mentions that evening had come (4:35; 6:47)—a signal that something significant is about to happen (1:32; 11:11, 19; 14:17; 15:42). Both trips also mention a common destination—'the other side', a foreign and unknown place. Here, it is a reference to actual foreign territory, but could it not also refer to the possibility that these men were journeying to a deeper understanding of God?

I wonder how Jesus felt that day in the boat, as the disciples challenged him about being uncaring. Then, as soon as the storm had calmed, he was seen not as uncaring but awesome—how very human and predictable!

Afterwards, Jesus wanted them to reflect on two things: fear and faith—and how they are connected. He wanted them to see and understand that God's kingdom is not a private affair for a small holy huddle, but wide open to all of humanity and the journey they were on was taking them into a new place in their relationship with God.

Reflection

Let us ponder, as the disciples did, the things that frighten us and remember that Jesus continues to offer faith as a gift to strengthen us, to calm the storms of our lives.

ANDREW JONES

Reinterpretation and misunderstanding

Then [Jesus] called the crowd again and said to them, 'Listen to me, all of you, and understand: there is nothing outside a person that by going in can defile, but the things that come out are what defile.' When he had left the crowd and entered the house, his disciples asked him about the parable. He said to them, 'Then do you also fail to understand?'

To make proper sense of this short passage, it is important to read the whole of chapter 7, as it fits into the wider controversy regarding purity laws. It begins with a challenge from the Pharisees and scribes regarding the disciples' failure to perform ritual washing before eating (vv. 1–8).

Jesus' criticism that his opponents are substituting their own traditions for God's commandments leads to the example of the practice of *Corban*—an Aramaic word for 'an offering' especially to God (vv. 9–13). The *Corban* vow involved consecrating one's property and resources to the temple. Once this vow was made, those assets belonged to the temple treasury and, although still in the hands of the owner, could not be used.

Finally, Jesus gives a public statement and a private explanation about the invalidity of the Jewish food laws (vv. 14–23). He rejects the Pharisaic tradition surrounding the laws' observance, and warns against substituting human teachings for divine commandments and using the law to escape from personal obligation. The implicit claim is that he is the authoritative interpreter of Old Testament law.

At issue is the Pharisees' oral tradition, known as *halakah*—an idea that linked back to the original revelation to Moses on Mount Sinai. The Pharisees claimed that there were two revelations on Mount Sinai—one written on the tablets of stone and one oral conversation later recorded in the *halakah*. It is this that Jesus is attacking here, but, once again, in private, the disciples ask him about the parable and his response suggests that there is a further lack of understanding on their part.

Reflection

Jesus challenges the boundaries imposed by the purity laws, judging who is 'in' and who is 'out'—the 'them' and 'us' syndrome—recognising such boundaries as protecting the privileged and preserving inequality.

ANDREW JONES

MARK 7:32–33, 36–37 (NRSV, ABRIDGED)

Don't tell them about me

> They brought to him a deaf man who had an impediment in his speech; and they begged him to lay his hand on him... [Jesus] spat and touched his tongue... Then Jesus ordered them to tell no one; but the more he ordered them, the more zealously they proclaimed it. They were astounded beyond measure, saying, 'He has done everything well; he even makes the deaf to hear and the mute to speak.'

Yesterday Jesus attacked the purity laws; today he continues that attack by using 'unclean' spittle to heal the man incapable of hearing and speaking properly (v. 33). His command that the crowd be silent about what they have seen suggests his ability to heal the sick was not the purpose of the story. He warned the crowd to keep secret what they had seen him do because, to make sense of it, there was more to come. Mark wanted to show that Jesus was much more than a healer and his full identity would be revealed only by the cross and resurrection.

Here, however, the prohibition has the opposite effect and the crowd's reaction witnesses to the reality of the cure, while underlining the theme of discovering Jesus' true identity. The words that express the crowd's enthusiasm (v. 37) are taken from a section of Isaiah, which presents a vision of Israel's glorious future (Isaiah 35:3–6). The use of this Old Testament text here indicates that Israel's glorious future is already present in the ministry of Jesus; in Jesus' activities the kingdom of God is present.

Jesus' message in this section of the Gospel is deeply radical and Mark's inclusion of the story of the man with speech and hearing difficulties is a recognition that people will find this message difficult to hear and even understand. There are no longer any privileged nations or groups or individuals—all are invited to come out of denial and into discipleship.

Reflection

All that was a long time ago and in a foreign land, but have things really changed? Would Jesus accuse us of not hearing and not understanding? Are our Christian communities inclusive of all? If not, what can we do?

ANDREW JONES

Don't show them what I can do

They came to Bethsaida. Some people brought a blind man to him
and begged him to touch him… Then Jesus laid his hands on [the
man's] eyes again; and he looked intently and his sight was
restored, and he saw everything clearly. Then he sent him away to
his home, saying, 'Do not even go into the village.'

If any story in Mark's Gospel has a symbolic function, it is the healing
of the blind man at Bethsaida. At this point, Jesus' ministry in Galilee
comes to a close and, along with his disciples, he travels towards
Jerusalem. On the journey, discussion focuses on instructing them
about his identity and what it really means to be a disciple. Significantly,
this section begins and ends with a healing of a blind man—symbolically stating that things are beginning to get clearer and eyes are opening to see the new order (8:22–26; 10:46–52).

In the case of the healing of the first blind man (our passage today),
the coming to sight is gradual and imperfect (8:24–25) and he does not
follow Jesus. In the second healing, Bartimaeus is healed immediately
and follows Jesus on the way. For me, the first healing represents a 'first
stage' of Jesus' intention of eradicating blindness. His healing touch is
only partially successful and the man requires a second in order to 'see
clearly' (8:25). The disciples' blindness will be lifted when they understand Jesus' teaching about the meaning of Christian discipleship and
his own suffering, death and resurrection.

We remember that Bethsaida was the place towards which Jesus and
his disciples embarked on their second major journey by boat in this
Gospel (6:45–53). The trip ended with Mark's first indication of the
disciples' blindness (6:52). We should also recall that the voyage was
unsuccessful—the group never actually arrived at Bethsaida. In this
event, that journey is now resolved—the 'blind' group of disciples
finally reach their destination and blindness is healed.

Reflection

*If the conversation before the boat trip (8:13) is a 'red light' to us
readers—a warning against reading 'blindly'—the healing in Bethsaida is
a 'green light' to continue in the quest for understanding!*

ANDREW JONES

More and more secrets

Jesus went on with his disciples to the village of Caesarea Philippi; and on the way he asked his disciples, 'Who do people say that I am?... But who do you say that I am?' Peter answered him, 'You are the Messiah.' And he sternly ordered them not to tell anyone about him.

Peter's confession of Jesus as the Messiah is pivotal in Mark's Gospel. Jesus and the disciples have come to the district of Caesarea Philippi, a major Hellenistic city. The action begins with Jesus suddenly turning and interrogating his disciples. Both his questions are to do with how he is perceived (vv. 27, 29) and raise serious concerns linked to the doubts about Jesus' identity, which have been lingering in the minds of his disciples (4:41) and also his opponents (6:3).

Peter's answer is momentous: it introduces the politically loaded term 'Messiah' (in Greek, *Christos*), the 'anointed one'. Jesus is not simply a great prophet; he is a royal figure who will restore the political fortunes of Israel. Thus, by his response, Peter is stating that revolution is at hand. He is immediately silenced by Jesus—and Mark uses the same word here as when Jesus silenced the demons (1:25; 3:12) and the wind (4:39). Jesus calls for silence to avoid any false interpretations of his messiahship, so that he can teach them what it really means (8:31).

If we read the section following this passage, we find it contains three crucial teachings to explain Jesus' true identity and take the story in a new direction—that is, the long march towards Jerusalem. The first crucial teaching (8:31—9:29) explains what it means to call Jesus 'Christ' and what its implications are for the disciples. The second (9:30—10:31) explores the theme of the kingdom of God and what entering it might demand. The third (10:32–45) consists of a third prediction of Jesus' suffering death, which is more detailed than the previous two (8:31; 9:31).

Reflection

From Bethsaida to Bartimaeus, Mark is serving us notice that we have arrived at the heart of an ideological conflict and raises a question for us: are we truly on the side of God?

ANDREW JONES

Even more questions

As they were coming down the mountain, [Jesus] ordered them to tell no one about what they had seen, until after the Son of Man had risen from the dead. So they kept the matter to themselves, questioning what this rising from the dead could mean.

There are two incidents involved in the transfiguration: the first (vv. 2–8) establishes Jesus' glorious identity as the beloved Son of God and the second (vv. 9–13) places his divine sonship in the context of Jewish expectations about the coming Kingdom and resurrection of the dead. Because the risen Christ never actually appears in Mark's Gospel, could this be a kind of 'preview' of the resurrection—a story of triumph, a crown to go with the coming cross?

The experience ends abruptly, however, and Jesus forbids the three disciples to declare what they have seen until after the resurrection. His warning is strong and direct (5:43 and 7:36), as if to shut down any opportunity to exalt the 'miracle' itself. It is kept secret because the disciples will not understand it until they have understood the meaning of resurrection. This has been Mark's point all along and to grasp that point means grasping the whole idea of secrecy in his Gospel.

The reality is that the disciples do not get it at this point. As they descended the mountain, what they probably struggled with most was how Jesus could be raised from the dead before the general resurrection at the coming of God's kingdom. Their puzzlement leads the discussion to Elijah (9:11–13). Malachi 4:5 stated clearly that Elijah must come before any kingdom is established, to turn the hearts of the people. Mark, however, already anticipated this (1:2) when he quoted Malachi 3:1 with reference to John the Baptist. Perhaps John was Mark's Elijah? He certainly preached repentance in order to turn the hearts of the people. Jesus concedes that Elijah must come first (Mark 9:12–13), but he also insists that his own passion and death will precede resurrection.

Reflection

The disciples regarded the transfiguration as a moment of glory to be commemorated; Jesus saw it as a necessary pause before turning towards Jerusalem and a preparation for the cross.

ANDREW JONES

Anonymity

They went on from there and passed through Galilee. [Jesus] did not want anyone to know it, for he was teaching his disciples, saying to them, 'The Son of Man is to be betrayed into human hands, and they will kill him, and three days after being killed, he will rise again.' But they did not understand what he was saying and were afraid to ask him.

We are still in that section of the Gospel where Jesus is offering three sets of teaching to reveal his true identity. What holds much of this teaching together is the theme of the kingdom of God and the radical demands that entering it might involve.

Today's passage opens the second of these sets, which begins with a prediction of Jesus' death and resurrection, but, once again, contains a call for secrecy. The reason for this is probably because Jesus needs more time and space to instruct his disciples about what will happen to him.

The theme of betrayal becomes more prominent as the Gospel moves towards Jerusalem and, I think, it is less a reference to what Judas did and more to do with the divine plan of salvation in which Jesus' death is pivotal. In none of Mark's predictions of the Passion (8:31; 9:31; 10:33–34), however, is the precise mode of Jesus' death made clear. Here, we may hear echoes of two verses in Daniel (7:25 and 12:2), which speak respectively of being delivered into the hands of rulers and the resurrection of the just.

Again, the disciples cannot grasp the meaning of this 'saying'. The Greek word used for 'saying' here only occurs twice in Mark's Gospel—the second time is when Peter remembers Jesus' prediction of his denial (14:72). Mark seems to be suggesting that betrayal is the consequence of failing to understand and accept the destiny of Jesus.

Reflection

The disciples seem to want to stick with the political meaning of Jesus as Messiah, hence they argue on the road about who is the greatest (9:33–37). Such obsession with power and status was anathema to Jesus—no wonder they were afraid to reveal their conversation to him!

ANDREW JONES

No answers, no details

Again they came to Jerusalem. As he was walking in the temple, the chief priests, the scribes, and the elders came to him and said, 'By what authority are you doing these things? Who gave you this authority to do them?' Jesus said to them, '... Did the baptism of John come from heaven, or was it of human origin?'... They answered Jesus, 'We do not know.' And Jesus said to them, 'Neither will I tell you by what authority I am doing these things.'

On the previous day, Jesus had created havoc in the temple when he dealt with the injustices of the money-changers. Today, as if he had never been there before, he returns to the temple in a calm, relaxed way. It was inevitable that he would be approached by the authorities and their question to him was designed to trap Jesus into a public admission that his authority was from God, thus laying the groundwork for a charge of blasphemy (14:64).

The chief priests, the scribes and the elders were, in effect, the first authority in the land. At that time, they were the first communal court of justice in the province and the highest Jewish court of justice. So, they represented the Jewish state, which, as Jesus predicted (8:31), would engineer his execution (14:43, 53; 15:1). They believed they were the 'earthly' authority that was legitimised in 'heaven', but, in Jesus' response to their question concerning his authority, he exposes this 'earth/heaven' issue as nonsense. He cites John the Baptist, asking a counter-question about the origin of John's authority. As John was killed by the political authorities who were threatened by his preaching of repentance, the question is a loaded one and their answer is, accordingly, non-committal. Jesus maintains that prophetic action is sanctioned either from the 'outside' or from 'within' the present social order. In as much as his opponents have not granted Jesus authority, it must have come from God.

Reflection

Jesus exposes the disunity of the religious authorities and their fear and mistrust of those they were supposed to serve. In our prayers today, let us ask God for integrity and honesty in leadership.

ANDREW JONES

One last question

As [Jesus] came out of the temple, one of his disciples said to him, 'Look, Teacher, what large stones and what large buildings!' Then Jesus asked him, 'Do you see these great buildings? Not one stone will be left here upon another, all will be thrown down.' When he was sitting on the Mount of Olives opposite the temple, Peter, James, John, and Andrew asked him privately, 'Tell us, when will this be, and what will be the sign that all these things are about to be accomplished?'

So we come to the opening of Jesus' final conversation with his disciples (13:1–37). There seems to be a tension here between his prediction about the destruction of the temple and the rest of the conversation, which concerns the end of the world. As we have come to expect, the tension is based on the fact that the disciples have once more missed the point. It is the amazement of one of them over the size and splendour of the temple buildings that gives Jesus the opportunity to make his pronouncement about its destruction.

In Mark's day, the temple had just recently been restored—a project begun almost a century earlier. By prophesying its destruction, Jesus stands in a long line of prophets saying the same thing (Micah 3:12; Jeremiah 26:18). His announcement that the temple will be destroyed will feature decisively in the Sanhedrin's prosecution of Jesus (Mark 14:58), as well as their taunts as he hangs on the cross (15:29).

What we see here is Jesus utterly repudiating the temple system. He now sets about warning his disciples against joining those who would wage a messianic war in its defence (13:14). Instead, he offers a vision of the end of the temple-based world and the dawn of a new one in which the powers of domination have been toppled.

Reflection

The keys to unlocking the messianic secret in Mark—the privacy, anonymity, misunderstanding, mystery and all the questions—are this final vision of the dawn of a new world and the cross and resurrection of Jesus as the means of achieving that new world.

ANDREW JONES

Supporting Messy Church with a gift in your will

For many charities, income from legacies is crucial in enabling them to plan ahead, and often provides the funding to develop new projects. Legacies make a significant difference to the ability of charities to achieve their purpose. In just this way, a legacy to support BRF's ministry would make a huge difference.

One of the fastest growing areas of BRF is its Messy Church ministry (www.messychurch.org.uk). Messy Church is a form of church focused on building relationships, engaging with people outside the usual church context and building a Christ-centred community. Messy Church gives families and all age groups an opportunity to be together and is a congregation in its own right. In addition, it is being delivered in a variety of different contexts in local communities, including care homes, prisons, inner cities, schools and rural areas. Week by week we are seeing new Messy Churches starting up across the UK and around the globe, across all major Christian denominations. A conservative estimate is that over 400,000 people are attending Messy Church each month.

Throughout its history, BRF's ministry has been enabled thanks to the generosity of those who have shared its vision and supported its work, both by giving during their lifetime and also through legacy gifts.

A legacy gift would help fund the development and sustainability of BRF's Messy Church ministry into the future. We hope you may consider a legacy gift to help us continue to take this work forward in the decades to come.

For further information about making a gift to BRF in your will or to discuss how a specific bequest could be used to develop our ministry, please contact Sophie Aldred (Head of Fundraising) or Richard Fisher (Chief Executive) by email at fundraising@brf.org.uk or by phone on 01865 319700.

This page is intentionally left blank.

The BRF

Magazine

Celebrating ten years of *Quiet Spaces*

Karen Laister

Spirituality is seen as a journey by many people, and it would be true to say that our prayer and spirituality journal *Quiet Spaces* **has been on a journey over these past ten years as it has evolved in both content and style.**

When we first started discussing the possibility of a journal that would help people experience a relational approach to their faith, we struggled to find a name. It took us much debate to decide that 'Quiet Spaces' was what we wanted to provide for its readers. *Quiet Spaces* was born out of a recognition that we need to create space to grow our relationship with God, to spend time with him and learn spiritual disciplines that aid our reflection and contemplation. Becky Winter, the first editor of *Quiet Spaces*, talked about wanting people to 'know God rather than knowing about God'.

We also envisaged the journal being very different from our Bible reading notes. In fact, we saw it sitting alongside *New Daylight*, *Guidelines* and *Day by Day with God*, complementing their approach and providing material to develop a life of prayer.

With *Quiet Spaces* we wanted to enable give readers a starting point to explore different styles of Christian spirituality and provide approaches to enrich a life of prayer and spirituality. Initially *Quiet Spaces* was unstructured and readers could dip in and out as they wished. More recently we have provided a structure based on different themes to enable people to use the journal on a regular basis if they wish.

'Be still and know that I am God' (Psalm 46:10, NIV) is a call to stop and discover God. Some of us might be good at doing this, while others can't seem to find the time or, when we do, find our minds floating off in all kinds of directions. Making time, in many respects, is the starting point for our prayer or communion with God, when we still ourselves and invite God to be in those moments. *Quiet Spaces* provides readings, reflection, creativity and prayers to explore spirituality in the stillness of our soul and to begin to glimpse something of God.

Quiet Spaces might be something that you keep alongside your Bible and dip into over the course of a four-month issue. There might be material that you keep returning to because you have been moved by a reflection, prayer or poem. It has captured your attention and draws you back to explore more. The eight or nine sections in each edition allow you to plan some longer periods of quiet. We sometimes have to be intentional about carving out time away from the demands and the noise of life for space with God or to give ourselves some much-needed rest. It is when we stop and reflect that we gain perspective, seeing God alongside us in the difficult, the mundane or the times of joy.

Christian spirituality throughout the ages has used techniques to stop and reflect. The 'examen' is a Jesuit approach to reviewing the day. We might not have time to do this daily, but perhaps every couple of weeks we can look back at the ways we have seen God in our lives since we last stopped to examine our faith journey. Keeping a journal might be useful if you are using *Quiet Spaces* as a mini retreat. Reflecting on what has taken place in your life allows you to consider situations that have upset or pleased you, then to think about how you could have approached things differently and to invite God to journey with you.

Alongside *Quiet Spaces*, BRF runs a Quiet Day programme and organises a Festival of Prayer each year with Oxford Diocese. Learning and sharing with others provides encouragement and can be a very special time. For information about our Quiet Day programme, you can visit our website: www.quietspaces.org.uk.

At the beginning of this article, I wrote that *Quiet Spaces* has been on a journey since its launch ten years ago, and we are grateful to Becky Winter, Naomi Starkey, Heather Fenton and the current editor, Sally Smith, for bringing together writers who have such wide experience in different aspects of spirituality.

One reader wrote to us recently, 'Along with *Guidelines*, this year I ordered a copy of *Quiet Spaces*. At first l wondered how l would find time to read another set of devotions, but it is proving a wonderful resource and l am trying to limit how much l read in one session, otherwise it will be read within a couple of weeks! I find the themes really make me be still before God and meditate on his word.' Another reader wrote, 'It is simply brilliant. Format and content are excellent.'

We couldn't hope for better accolades to endorse *Quiet Spaces*. If you would like to try it, please visit www.biblereadingnotes.org.uk/quiet-spaces/ and click on 'Order a sample copy'. Then enter the promotion code QSSAMPLE at the checkout. Alternatively, contact the BRF office on 01865 319700 to order your free sample, quoting QSSAMPLE.

Karen Laister is Deputy Chief Executive of BRF.

BRF needs your help!

Sophie Aldred

Over the past decade or so, BRF's charitable activities have expanded from publishing Bible reading notes and books into exciting new and complementary areas such as the Barnabas in Schools programme, Messy Church and, most recently, The Gift of Years.

BRF's charitable activities resource:

- Christian growth and the understanding of the Bible by individuals of all ages
- churches for outreach in the local community
- the teaching of Christianity and the Bible within primary schools
- children's and family ministry in churches

Our main priority is to make what we have to offer widely accessible, and to make a difference in the lives of individuals, communities, schools and churches. BRF's charitable activities are funded partly through income generated from sales of resources and fees from training and events, and partly through voluntary income from donations, grants and legacies.

The following specific activities are funded primarily by donations, grants and legacies:

Messy Church

The Messy Church network continues to expand, with the number of Messy Churches listed in the directory on www.messychurch.org.uk growing on a daily basis. As a way of resourcing churches to reach out to and engage with those particularly beyond the fringe of the church family, it continues to make a significant impact on local communities throughout the UK and in 20 other countries. With its emphasis on fun, craft, celebration and eating together, Messy Church has proved to be a way of 'being church' that works in many different situations—rural, urban and suburban, with large and small church congregations and across the denominations.

Who Let The Dads Out?

Who Let The Dads Out?'s vision is to 'turn the hearts of fathers to their children and the hearts of children to their fathers' (Malachi 4:6). It is an extremely effective way for churches to engage with fathers and father figures of pre-school-aged children—particularly those with whom the church has very little, if any, contact. Who Let The Dads Out? groups across the UK are providing a vital catalyst for churches to engage with fathers and father figures, and a context to begin to explore issues and questions around fatherhood and faith.

The Gift of Years

The Gift of Years is BRF's newest initiative, which we started to develop in 2014. In recent years, Debbie Thrower (former BBC and ITV journalist and presenter) has developed a highly effective model for community-based 'Anna Chaplaincy' to older people in Alton, Hampshire. BRF enbraced the 'Anna Chaplain' model as the centrepiece of a new ministry, The Gift of Years, whose vision is 'resourcing the spiritual journey of older people'. Through this we are seeking both to resource older people themselves and also to resource ministry among older people, wherever they may be—in congregations, in residential care, in their own homes and in the community.

Barnabas in Schools

Barnabas in Schools is a professional education service to primary schools, helping teachers and pupils alike to explore Christianity and the Bible creatively within RE and Collective Worship. We do this through Barnabas RE Days, specialist In-Service Training (INSET) sessions for teachers, published resources for the classroom, and a website providing a wealth of support materials and ideas available to download. We estimate that the team works with 45,000 primary school children each year. Funding for RE is very limited in many primary schools, so the fees for Barnabas RE Days and INSET sessions are set at a level to make them as affordable as possible.

Foundations21

Foundations21 (www.foundations21.net) is BRF's free online Christian lifelong learning resource, offering a wealth of material to explore and enabling individuals and small groups to grow in their faith and discipleship. We continue to develop and refine this resource, and are currently working on an entry-level Christian learning app for tablet and mobile phone users.

Barnabas in Churches

For 20 years BRF has been resourcing ministry among children and families in churches through our websites and published resources, enabling children under 11, and the adults that work with them, to explore Christianity creatively and bring the Bible alive. The Barnabas in Churches website (www.barnabasinchurches.org.uk) provides a wealth of free downloadable ideas for children's leaders to use with their Sunday or midweek groups, alongside the wide range of books published under our Barnabas for Children imprint to resource, equip and inspire them in their ministry.

Faith in Homes

Through our Faith in Homes initiative and its website, we are helping families to explore the Christian faith and to find God in the everyday at home, with ideas, articles, advice, published resources and workshops. Visit www.faithinhomes.org.uk.

Could you help us?

Messy Church, Who Let The Dads Out?, The Gift of Years, Barnabas in Schools, Foundations21, Barnabas in Churches and Faith in Homes are all funded primarily through donations, grants and legacies. We need your help to continue the growth and development of BRF's work in these areas.

Ways you could help:
- Give a personal donation (see page 151 for further details)
- Encourage your church to support BRF as part of its regular giving
- Make a legacy gift to BRF in your will
- Pray for everyone involved in BRF: the trustees and the staff team

Sophie Aldred is Head of Fundraising at BRF.

Recommended reading

Kevin Ball

Why do you read books? To escape, to learn? To deepen your faith? For me, the beauty of books is the way they show you new sides to a coin, opening up new possibilities and new understanding.

Tony Horsfall's new book, *Deep Calls to Deep*, asks, 'Is suffering an inescapable part of the journey towards knowing God?' It's tough, but true, that faith is shown for what it is in the hardest times, the messy times of life. Tony looks at the psalms of lament, songs that were written in the tough times, to see how the writers work through their messy life situations in a way that strengthens and develops their faith. You can read an extract from the book in the following pages.

What new understanding for our faith can we find in football? Who Let The Dads Out? founder Mark Chester reflects on the beautiful game, his family's love of Liverpool FC and his stuttering attempts to become a professional (well—good amateur!) player as he invites you to train with him (reflectively, that is) to discover the soul of the game.

How do I discover my true vocation? That's the question at the heart of Katy Magdalene Price's new book, *I Think It's God Calling*. Through her amusing and witty style, Katy shares her true story of how she discovered that God was calling her to ordained ministry, even though she struggled to believe in God.

For those in church leadership, we are pleased to be publishing *Pioneering a New Future* from the Archbishops' Missioner and Fresh Expressions Team Leader, Canon Phil Potter. Phil helps leaders to understand the changing church scene, with the emerging and growth of fresh expressions of church, charting a positive course through change to embrace these new missional possibilities. This is a revised and updated edition of *The Challenge of Change*, which we published in 2009.)

You can read sample chapters from all of the books described below at www.brfonline.org.uk.

Deep Calls to Deep
Spiritual formation in the hard places of life
Tony Horsfall

Tony explains his interest in the psalms of lament and their usefulness in spiritual formation.

It seems to me that the book of Psalms, when taken as a whole, provides us with a wonderful handbook on spiritual formation. Here we see life with God as it really is. True, there is a certain distance between us and the psalms—historically, geographically, culturally and even theologically, as they reflect the old covenant between God and his people. Not everything we read sits easily with a contemporary Western mindset. They are both familiar and foreign to us, yet they continue to speak deeply to us about our relationship with God. As one Old Testament professor puts it:

As we read the Psalms, we are entering into the sanctuary, the place where God meets men and women in a special way. We will see that the conversation between God and his people is direct, intense, intimate, and above all, honest. Thus, the Psalms are a kind of literary sanctuary in the Scripture. The place where God meets his people in a special way, where his people may address him with their praise and lament.'

It was this intimacy with God, this raw honesty with him, that drew me to the psalms in a fresh way. They give us words to use with God in our moments of joy and victory (praise) and in our times of despair and defeat (lament). As we read them, we can make the words our own, enter into the experience of the writer and find our own voice before God. In particular, I was drawn to the songs of lament, prayers that come from a deep place and reflect the struggle to understand what God is doing in our lives.

These 'sad songs' make up nearly a third of all the psalms and yet they are mostly neglected by the church today. Much of our spirituality is geared toward relieving our pain and finding ways to ensure happiness, success and well-being… Yet struggle and challenge are necessary for authentic spiritual growth. The reality is that God sometimes does lead us down difficult paths as he seeks to draw us closer to himself and form his life within us…

978 1 84101 731 0, pb, 160 pages, £7.99

I Think It's God Calling
A vocation diary
Katy Magdalene Price

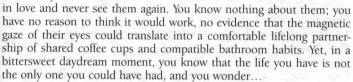

Katy shares the emotional and spiritual ups and downs of her calling to the priesthood, as well as the challenges for family and friends arising from such a major life change.

Vocation is a malady that runs its course differently in different people... For me, it felt a bit like this: you meet someone on a train and fall in love and never see them again. You know nothing about them; you have no reason to think it would work, no evidence that the magnetic gaze of their eyes could translate into a comfortable lifelong partnership of shared coffee cups and compatible bathroom habits. Yet, in a bittersweet daydream moment, you know that the life you have is not the only one you could have had, and you wonder...

  I knew nothing about priesthood... Priesthood was not an ambition, a plan or even a desire; it was the last thing I wanted... But somehow all the sensible answers sounded false. It was also getting increasingly hard to hide from other people. People you'd never expect seemed to be picking up on some 'vibe'. A jolly homeless guy who usually spoke in a succession of unintelligible bad puns broke into what sounded like prophecy. Even my mother, who had finally given up her long-cherished hope that I would become a writer (hi Mum!), tentatively suggested that I might make a career out of being 'interested in religion'...

978 1 84101 645 0, pb, 176 pages, £7.99

The Soul of Football
One man's story of football, family and faith
Mark Chester

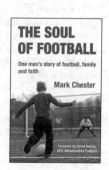

Cloning Jamie Carragher, Lionel Messi's mistakes and 'It's all Wayne Rooney's fault' are just three of the issues Mark reflects on as he shares his love of all things things footy and how love for the beautiful game can help football fans begin to discover the victory of a Christian faith. Mark writes:

It was a dream I shared with the vast majority of other boys and men. The dream was fuelled by Subbuteo and *Match of the Day*, by Panini stickers and *Football Focus*, by *Match* magazine and football cards with flat, rigid pieces of bubble gum so sharp you could cut yourself if you put them into your mouth at the wrong angle. But most of all, it was a dream fuelled by a man called Roy Race of Melchester Rovers...

'This book gets beyond the surface of football, and reminds us that we need to get beyond the surface of life, too.' (Revd John K. Boyers, Chaplain, Manchester United)

978 1 84101 654 2, pb, 112 pages, £6.99

Pioneering a new future
A guide to shaping change and changing the shape of church
Phil Potter

Change can be a frightening thing, particularly for leaders and congregations not fully prepared for what it will mean. The author of *The Challenge of Cell Church*, which has sold over 10,000 copies, returns in this revised edition of *The Challenge of Change*, offering a map for healthy and godly change in the local church. Writing as a pastor and practitioner, Phil explains ways of shaping change of any kind in the life of a church and presents a guide to understanding the changing shape of church, in particular the 'fresh expressions' of church now emerging. He uses his experiences of leading his own church through five major transition periods, with his own mistakes and personal stories as examples to illustrate his points.

Pioneering a New Future is ideal for church leaders of any denomination wanting to take their congregations through change. It is also ideal for church members preparing to embark on a particular project or simply wanting to be equipped for whatever lies ahead. It speaks to reluctant traditionalists and impatient visionaries, to both struggling and thriving congregations. Also included are over 100 questions for personal and group reflection.

978 0 85746 414 9, pb, 176 pages, £7.99 (available September 2015)

To order copies of any of these books, please turn to the order form on page 155, or visit www.brfonline.org.uk.

SUPPORTING BRF'S MINISTRY

As a Christian charity, BRF is involved in eight complementary areas.

- **BRF** (www.brf.org.uk) resources adults for their spiritual journey through Bible reading notes, books and Quiet Days. BRF also provides the infrastructure that supports our other specialist ministries.
- **Foundations21** (www.foundations21.net) provides flexible and innovative ways for individuals and groups to explore their Christian faith and discipleship through a multimedia internet-based resource.
- **Messy Church** (www.messychurch.org.uk), led by Lucy Moore, enables churches all over the UK (and increasingly abroad) to reach children and adults beyond the fringes of the church.
- **Barnabas in Churches** (www.barnabasinchurches.org.uk) helps churches to support, resource and develop their children's ministry with the under-11s more effectively .
- **Barnabas in Schools** (www.barnabasinschools.org.uk) enables primary school children and teachers to explore Christianity creatively and bring the Bible alive within RE and Collective Worship.
- **Faith in Homes** (www.faithinhomes.org.uk) supports families to explore and live out the Christian faith at home.
- **Who Let The Dads Out** (www.wholetthedadsout.org) inspires churches to engage with dads and their pre-school children.
- **The Gift of Years** (www.brf.org.uk/thegiftofyears) celebrates the blessings of long life and seeks to meet the spiritual needs of older people.

At the heart of BRF's ministry is a desire to equip adults and children for Christian living—helping them to read and understand the Bible, explore prayer and grow as disciples of Jesus. We need your help to make an impact on the local church, local schools and the wider community.

- You could support BRF's ministry with a one-off gift or regular donation (using the response form on page 153).
- You could consider making a bequest to BRF in your will.
- You could encourage your church to support BRF as part of your church's giving to home mission—perhaps focusing on a specific area of our ministry, or a particular member of our Barnabas team.
- Most important of all, you could support BRF with your prayers.

If you would like to discuss how a specific gift or bequest could be used in the development of our ministry, please phone 01865 319700 or mail enquiries@brf.org.uk.

Whatever you can do or give, we thank you for your support.

BRF has been helping individuals connect with the Bible for over 90 years. We want to support churches as they seek to encourage church members into regular Bible reading.

Order a Bible reading resources pack

This pack is designed to give your church the tools to publicise our Bible reading notes. It includes:

- Sample Bible reading notes for your congregation to try.
- Publicity resources, including a poster.
- A church magazine feature about Bible reading notes.

The pack is free, but we welcome a £5 donation to cover the cost of postage. If you require a pack to be sent outside the UK or require a specific number of sample Bible reading notes, please contact us for postage costs. More information about what the current pack contains is available on our website.

How to order and find out more

- Visit www.biblereadingnotes.org.uk/for-churches/
- Telephone BRF on 01865 319700 between 9.15 am and 5.30 pm.
- Write to us at BRF, 15 The Chambers, Vineyard, Abingdon, OX14 3FE

Keep informed about our latest initiatives

We are continuing to develop resources to help churches encourage people into regular Bible reading, wherever they are on their journey. Join our email list at www.biblereadingnotes.org.uk/helpingchurches/ to stay informed about the latest initiatives that your church could benefit from.

Introduce a friend to our notes

We can send information about our notes and current prices for you to pass on. Please contact us.

BRF MINISTRY APPEAL RESPONSE FORM

I want to help BRF by funding some of its core ministries. Please use my gift for:

☐ Where most needed ☐ Barnabas Children's Ministry ☐ Foundations21
☐ Messy Church ☐ Who Let The Dads Out? ☐ The Gift of Years

Please complete all relevant sections of this form and print clearly.

Title _____ First name/initials _____ Surname _____

Address _____

_____ Postcode _____

Telephone _____ Email _____

Regular giving

If you would like to give by direct debit, please tick the box below and fill in details:

☐ I would like to make a regular gift of £ _____ per month / quarter / year
(delete as appropriate) by Direct Debit. (Please complete the form on page 159.)

If you would like to give by standing order, please contact Debra McKnight (tel: 01865 319700; email debra.mcknight@brf.org.uk; write to BRF address).

One-off donation

Please accept my special gift of

☐ £10 ☐ £50 ☐ £100 (other) £ _____ by

☐ Cheque / Charity Voucher payable to 'BRF'
☐ Visa / Mastercard / Charity Card
(delete as appropriate)

Name on card _____

Card no. ☐☐☐☐ ☐☐☐☐ ☐☐☐☐ ☐☐☐☐

Start date ☐☐ ☐☐   Expiry date ☐☐ ☐☐

Security code ☐☐☐

Signature _____ Date _____

☐ I would like to give a legacy to BRF. Please send me further information.

☐ I want BRF to claim back tax on this gift.
(If you tick this box, please fill in gift aid declaration overleaf.)

Please detach and send this completed form to: BRF, 15 The Chambers, Vineyard, Abingdon OX14 3FE.
BRF is a Registered Charity (No.233280)

GIFT AID DECLARATION

Bible Reading Fellowship

Please treat as Gift Aid donations all qualifying gifts of money made
today ☐   in the past 4 years ☐   in the future ☐   (tick all that apply)

I confirm I have paid or will pay an amount of Income Tax and/or Capital Gains Tax for each tax year (6 April to 5 April) that is at least equal to the amount of tax that all the charities that I donate to will reclaim on my gifts for that tax year. I understand that other taxes such as VAT or Council Tax do not qualify. I understand the charity will reclaim 25p of tax on every £1 that I give on or after 6 April 2008.

Donor's details

Title _____ First name or initials _____ Surname _____

Full home address _____

_____

Postcode _____

Date _____

Signature _____

Please notify Bible Reading Fellowship if you:

- want to cancel this declaration
- change your name or home address
- no longer pay sufficient tax on your income and/or capital gains.

If you pay Income Tax at the higher or additional rate and want to receive the additional tax relief due to you, you must include all your Gift Aid donations on your Self-Assessment tax return or ask HM Revenue and Customs to adjust your tax code.

ND021

BRF PUBLICATIONS ORDER FORM

Please send me the following book(s):

	Quantity	Price	Total
731 0 Deep Calls to Deep (*T. Horsfall*)	_____	£7.99	_____
645 0 I Think It's God Calling (*K. Magdalene Price*)	_____	£7.99	_____
654 2 The Soul of Football (*M. Chester*)	_____	£6.99	_____
414 9 Pioneering a New Future (*P. Potter*)	_____	£7.99	_____
323 4 Living Liturgies (*C. George*)	_____	£7.99	_____
413 2 The Gift of Years (Bible reading notes)	_____	£2.50	_____
Quiet Spaces sample copy	_____	FREE	_____

Total cost of books £ _____
Donation £ _____
Postage and packing £ _____
TOTAL £ _____

POSTAGE AND PACKING CHARGES				
Order value	UK	Europe	Economy (Surface)	Standard (Air)
Under £7.00	£1.25	£3.00	£3.50	£5.50
£7.00–£29.00	£2.25	£5.50	£6.50	£10.00
£30.00 and over	free	prices on request		

Please complete the payment details below and send with payment to: **BRF, 15 The Chambers, Vineyard, Abingdon OX14 3FE**

Name _____

Address _____

_____ Postcode _____

Tel _____ Email _____

Total enclosed £ _____ (cheques should be made payable to 'BRF')

Please charge my Visa ❏ Mastercard ❏ Switch card ❏ with £ _____

Card no: ☐☐☐☐☐☐☐☐☐☐☐☐☐☐☐☐☐☐☐☐

Expires ☐☐☐☐ Security code ☐☐☐

Issue no (Switch only) ☐☐☐☐

Signature (essential if paying by credit/Switch) _____

NEW DAYLIGHT INDIVIDUAL SUBSCRIPTIONS

❏ I would like to take out a subscription myself:

Your name _____

Your address _____

_____

_____ Postcode _____

Tel _____ Email _____

Please send *New Daylight* beginning with the September 2015 / January 2016 / May 2016 issue: (delete as applicable)

(please tick box)

	UK	Europe/Economy	Standard
NEW DAYLIGHT	❏ £16.35	❏ £24.00	❏ £27.60
NEW DAYLIGHT 3-year sub	❏ £42.75		
NEW DAYLIGHT DELUXE	❏ £20.70	❏ £32.70	❏ £37.95
NEW DAYLIGHT daily email only	❏ £12.90 (UK and overseas)		

Please complete the payment details below and send with appropriate payment to: **BRF, 15 The Chambers, Vineyard, Abingdon OX14 3FE**

Total enclosed £ _____ (cheques should be made payable to 'BRF')

Please charge my Visa ❏ Mastercard ❏ Switch card ❏ with £ _____

Card no: ☐☐☐☐ ☐☐☐☐ ☐☐☐☐ ☐☐☐☐

Expires ☐☐☐☐ Security code ☐☐☐

Issue no (Switch only) ☐☐☐☐

Signature (essential if paying by card) _____

To set up a direct debit, please also complete the form on page 159 and send it to BRF with this form.

BRF is a Registered Charity

ND02

NEW DAYLIGHT GIFT SUBSCRIPTIONS

❏ I would like to give a gift subscription (please provide both names and addresses:

Your name _____

Your address _____

_____ Postcode _____

Tel _____ Email _____

Gift subscription name _____

Gift subscription address _____

_____ Postcode _____

Gift message (20 words max. or include your own gift card for the recipient)

_____

_____

Please send *New Daylight* beginning with the September 2015 / January 2016 / May 2016 issue: (delete as applicable)

(please tick box)

	UK	Europe/Economy	Standard
NEW DAYLIGHT	❏ £16.35	❏ £24.00	❏ £27.60
NEW DAYLIGHT 3-year sub	❏ £42.75		
NEW DAYLIGHT DELUXE	❏ £20.70	❏ £32.70	❏ £37.95
NEW DAYLIGHT daily email only	❏ £12.90 (UK and overseas)		

Please complete the payment details below and send with appropriate payment to: **BRF, 15 The Chambers, Vineyard, Abingdon OX14 3FE**

Total enclosed £ _____ (cheques should be made payable to 'BRF')

Please charge my Visa ❏ Mastercard ❏ Switch card ❏ with £ _____

Card no: ☐☐☐☐☐☐☐☐☐☐☐☐☐☐☐☐☐☐☐

Expires ☐☐☐☐ Security code ☐☐☐

Issue no (Switch only) ☐☐☐☐

Signature (essential if paying by card) _____

To set up a direct debit, please also complete the form on page 159 and send to BRF with this form.

DIRECT DEBIT PAYMENTS

Now you can pay for your annual subscription to BRF notes using Direct Debit. You need only give your bank details once, and the payment is made automatically every year until you cancel it. If you would like to pay by Direct Debit, please use the form opposite, entering your BRF account number under 'Reference'.

You are fully covered by the Direct Debit Guarantee:

The Direct Debit Guarantee

- This Guarantee is offered by all banks and building societies that accept instructions to pay Direct Debits.
- If there are any changes to the amount, date or frequency of your Direct Debit, The Bible Reading Fellowship will notify you 10 working days in advance of your account being debited or as otherwise agreed. If you request The Bible Reading Fellowship to collect a payment, confirmation of the amount and date will be given to you at the time of the request.
- If an error is made in the payment of your Direct Debit, by The Bible Reading Fellowship or your bank or building society, you are entitled to a full and immediate refund of the amount paid from your bank or building society.
  - – If you receive a refund you are not entitled to, you must pay it back when The Bible Reading Fellowship asks you to.
- You can cancel a Direct Debit at any time by simply contacting your bank or building society. Written confirmation may be required. Please also notify us.

The Bible Reading Fellowship

Instruction to your bank or building society to pay by Direct Debit

Please fill in the whole form using a ballpoint pen and send to The Bible Reading Fellowship, 15 The Chambers, Vineyard, Abingdon OX14 3FE.

Service User Number: | 5 | 5 | 8 | 2 | 2 | 9 |

Name and full postal address of your bank or building society

To: The Manager   Bank/Building Society

Address

                                    Postcode

Name(s) of account holder(s)

Branch sort code

| | | | | | |

Bank/Building Society account number

| | | | | | | | |

Reference

| | | | | | |

Instruction to your Bank/Building Society

Please pay The Bible Reading Fellowship Direct Debits from the account detailed in this instruction, subject to the safeguards assured by the Direct Debit Guarantee. I understand that this instruction may remain with The Bible Reading Fellowship and, if so, details will be passed electronically to my bank/building society.

Signature(s)

Date

Banks and Building Societies may not accept Direct Debit instructions for some types of account.

This page is intentionally left blank.